YOUR KNOWLEDGE HAS

- We will publish your bachelor's and master's thesis, essays and papers

- Your own eBook and book - sold worldwide in all relevant shops

- Earn money with each sale

Upload your text at www.GRIN.com and publish for free

Timo Schlichting

Fundamental Analysis, Behavioral Finance and Technical Analysis on the Stock Market

Theoretical Concepts and Their Practical Synthesis Capabilities

GRIN Verlag

Bibliografische Information der Deutschen Nationalbibliothek:

Die Deutsche Bibliothek verzeichnet diese Publikation in der Deutschen National-
bibliografie; detaillierte bibliografische Daten sind im Internet über http://dnb.d-
nb.de/ abrufbar.

Imprint:

Copyright © 2008 GRIN Verlag GmbH
Druck und Bindung: Books on Demand GmbH, Norderstedt Germany
ISBN: 978-3-640-37782-4

This book at GRIN:

http://www.grin.com/en/e-book/132302/fundamental-analysis-behavioral-finance-
and-technical-analysis-on-the

GRIN - Your knowledge has value

Der GRIN Verlag publiziert seit 1998 wissenschaftliche Arbeiten von Studenten, Hochschullehrern und anderen Akademikern als eBook und gedrucktes Buch. Die Verlagswebsite www.grin.com ist die ideale Plattform zur Veröffentlichung von Hausarbeiten, Abschlussarbeiten, wissenschaftlichen Aufsätzen, Dissertationen und Fachbüchern.

Visit us on the internet:

http://www.grin.com/

http://www.facebook.com/grincom

http://www.twitter.com/grin_com

FOM Fachhochschule für Oekonomie & Management
Duesseldorf
&
Avans+
Breda

Study Program in
Diplom-Kaufmann (FH),
Bachelor of Business Administration

Diploma Thesis / Bachelor Thesis
in partial submission of the Degree in
Diplom-Kaufmann (FH),
Bachelor of Business Administration

Fundamental Analysis, Behavioral Finance and
Technical Analysis on the Stock Market -
Theoretical Concepts and Their Practical Synthesis
Capabilities

Author: Timo Schlichting
               7th Semester

Leverkusen, DEC 13-2008

Table of Contents

List of Abbreviations

APT	Arbitrage Pricing Theory
APV	Adujsted Present Value
CAPM	Capital Asset Pricing Model
C-DAX	Composite-DAX
DAX	Deutscher Aktienindex
DCF	Discounted Cash Flow
EBT	Earnings before Taxes
EBIT	Earnings before Interests and Taxes
EBITDA	Earnings before Interests, Taxes, Depreciations and Amortisations
EMH	Efficient Market Hypothesis
FCF	Free Cash Flow
FTE	Flow to Equity
IDW	Institut Deutscher Wirtschaftsprüfer
Ifo	Institut für Wirtschaftsforschung
ISIN	International Securities Identification Number
MACD	Moving Average Convergence Divergences
PBR	Price Book Value Ratio
PEG	Price Earnings to Growth
ROE	Return on Equity
RSI	Relative Strength Index
RV	Residential Value
TC	Total Capital
Tr	Tax rate
SVAR	Structural Vector Autoregressive
SWOT	Strengths Weaknesses Opportunities Threats
VAR	Value at Risk
WACC	Weighted Average Cost of Capital
WpHG	Wertpapierhandelsgesetz

List of Figures

List of Tables

1. Introduction

During the last eleven months, the stock market has been characterized by crashes and a historically high volatility. In comparison to their peaks at the end of 2007, the Dow Jones Industrial Average Index and the DAX performance index have dropped almost 50% in value. The newspaper headlines around the world documented the extent of the stock market decrease and this historically high volatility:

"Wave of profit warnings expected – European groups face earnings fall out 40%" (Financial Times 2008a), "Porsche intentions baffle markets – Hedge funds scramble to assess damage" (Financial Times 2008c). Stock market analysts questioned whether "equity markets reached fair value?" (Financial Times 2008b) and partially drew the conclusion that "We're getting to a point now with valuations where shares are incredibly low – we haven't seen these levels since the 1930s." (Financial Times 2008d)

Considering these statements, the following two questions are raised: What is the "fair" value of a stock? And by which analysis concepts could stock market investors be enabled to evaluate, if stocks are worth buying or if they should be sold?

In order to be able to answer these questions, three general analysis concepts have been developed: fundamental analysis, behavioral finance and technical analysis. Historically considered, fundamental and technical analyses have always competed, often leading to advocates that ideologically judge either a fundamental analysis or technical analysis to be the one and only analyzing concept. Behavioral finance is a relatively new scientific approach to explain psychological anomalies on the stock market, but is also more and more often considered to be able to compete with both fundamental and technical analyses.

Still, do these analysis concepts really compete in practice or could they actually supplement each other with their respective strengths?

Taking the turbulent stock market phases as well as these unanswered questions about fundamental analysis, behavioral finance and the technical analysis into consideration, this thesis ultimately pursues two general objectives:

Firstly, fundamental analysis, behavioral finance and technical analysis should be scientifically examined in terms of their premises, analysis approaches, empirical evidences as well as strengths and weaknesses.

Secondly, it should be examined as to whether the fundamental analysis, behavioral finance and technical analysis have theoretical and practical synthesis capabilities that could be used for developing a synthesis concept. The synthesis concept should combine the respective strengths and eliminate the respective weaknesses of each of the three analysis concepts.

Taking these two objectives into consideration, the thesis follows the following procedure: the second chapter deals with the question of how efficient the stock market is. Considering that the predictive capabilities of the three analysis concepts are based on different efficiency assumptions, the stock market efficiency must be discussed first.

Afterwards, the fundamental analysis (see Chapter 3.), behavioral finance (see Chapter 4.) and technical analysis (see Chapter 5.) are examined in detail. The procedure required to guarantee an objective evaluation of the respective analysis concept always remains the same: at first, the definitions as well as the premises of the respective analysis concept are explained. Afterwards the most important analysis approaches are examined. In addition to that, empirical studies should prove if, and by which approaches, the analysis concept is able to predict future stock prices. In order to be able to develop a synthesis concept, each analysis concept is evaluated by a SWOT analysis, pursuing the objective of determining the respective strengths, weaknesses, opportunities and threats of the analysis concept being considered. At the end of each chapter, a preliminary conclusion is drawn, enabling the reader to follow the most important insights of each chapter.

Based on the previous SWOT analyses, the sixth chapter examines the synthesis capabilities of the fundamental analysis, behavioral finance and technical analysis. In a first step, the synthesis capabilities are theoretically analyzed (see Section 6.2.). Based on the theoretical consideration, the synthesis capabilities are also practically examined in a second step (see Section 6.3.). A broad empirical study using the example of the DAX performance index analyzes the predictive capabilities of the three analysis concepts. By evaluating the theoretical as well as the practical synthesis capabilities, a general conclusion is drawn about the synthesis capabilities (see Section 6.4.).

At the end of this thesis, a final conclusion as well as an outlook is developed, dealing with the realizations about the respective analysis concept as well as the cognitions and future opportunities of the developed synthesis concept (see Chapter 7.).

2. Information Efficiency on the Stock Market

2.1. Efficient Market Hypothesis

2.1.1. Definition and Theoretical Assumptions

Based on the assumptions of the expected utility theory (Morgenstern/von Neumann 1944) and the concept of rational expectations (Muth 1961), Fama developed the Efficient Market Hypothesis (EMH), which is currently one of the cornerstones of important neoclassical capital market models such as CAPM and APT (Cesar 1996, Schäfer and Vater 2002).

The EMH comes to the conclusion that "a market in which prices fully reflect available information is called efficient" (Fama 1970, p.383). "Fully reflect" means that "prices adjust rapidly and unbiased to new information" (Gonedes 1976, p. 612). Prices, therefore, only alter when new information is received by rational investors (Peters 1996). Information that is known by rational investors has already been processed by those and is therefore correctly reflected by the actual stock prices (Widdel 1996). Thus, future stock price movements are only effected by new fundamental information.

By definition, new information is surprising and unpredictable for the investor, making future information and thus, future stock prices, follow a random walk (Dressendörfer 1999). On the one hand, random walk means that future stock price changes are independent from previous stock price changes. On the other hand, random walk also means that future stock price changes are distributed normally (Dressendörfer 1999). According to Malkiel (1999, p.24), random walk therefore "means that short-run changes in stock prices cannot be predicted. Investment advisory services, earnings predictions, and complicated chart patterns are useless." But is this conclusion really indicative of reality for all of the three analysis concepts?

To be able to answer this question, the EMH is differentiated by its three efficiency forms in the following (Section 2.1.2.). Based on that differentiation, the three analysis concepts – fundamental analysis, behavioral finance and technical analysis – are classified in terms of their respective efficiency assumptions (Section 2.1.3.)

2.1.2. Efficiency Forms

According to Roberts, Fama classified the concept of information efficiency in three different forms of efficiency (Sapusek 1998). The efficiency forms differ in terms of their respective available information, whereby the stronger efficiency form contains the respective weaker efficiency form (Shleifer 2000):

- Weak form of information efficiency:
  The weak form of information efficiency is present if all of the information about the previous stock prices is contained in the actual stock market prices at any time.

- Semi-strong form of information efficiency:
  The semi-strong form of information efficiency is present if all public information is contained in the actual stock market prices at any time.

- Strong form of information efficiency:
  The strong form of information efficiency is present if all possible information – which includes insider information – is contained in the actual stock market prices at any given time.

2.1.3. Classification of Fundamental Analysis, Behavioral Finance and Technical Analysis

The distinction between the three forms of information efficiency is particularly important in terms of the applicability of the three analysis concepts – fundamental analysis, behavioral finance and technical analysis – which differ in their assumptions of their underlying information efficiency form (Sapusek 1998):

- Technical Analysis:
  This approach is based on the idea of analyzing historical stock prices in order to be able to draw conclusions on the future stock price movements (Brunnermeier 2001). Thus, technical analysis is based on an information efficiency assumption that is at least weaker than the weak form of information efficiency (Aronson 2007, Dornbusch 1998).
  Otherwise, the investor would not be able to generate steady abnormal returns by applying technical analysis, because all of the information about

the historical stock prices is already contained in the actual stock prices
(Aronson 2007, Menz 2004, Niquet 1997).

- Fundamental Analysis:
  This approach tries to generate an abnormal return by analyzing fundamental
  factors of a company to be able to draw a comparison between the
  theoretically justified fair value of a company's stock and the actual stock
  market price (Damodaran 2006). These fundamental factors are derived by
  analyzing public information – e.g. annual reports, macroeconomic indicators,
  etc.
  Unlike the technical approach, the fundamental analysis is able to generate
  an abnormal return, even if the weak form of information efficiency exists
  (Sapusek 1998). However, fundamental analysis requires at least one weaker
  form than the semi-strong form of information efficiency (Dornbusch 1998).
  Otherwise, the investor would not be able to generate steady abnormal
  returns by applying the fundamental analysis, because all public information
  is already correctly processed by the stock market and therefore, correctly
  reflected by the actual stock market prices (Haugen 1999).

- Behavioral Finance:
  The behavioral finance approach is based on the idea that investors do not
  behave rationally, but rather recurrently irrational (Shleifer 2000).
  In contrast to this, the EMH is based on the expected utility theory as well as
  the concept of rational expectations (Ellenrieder 2001). Thus, behavioral
  finance denies all three forms of information efficiency, because it denies the
  general concept of the EMH. This is due to the fact that it is based on
  completely different assumptions about the investors' behavior – e.g.
  irrationalities, like reacting biased and timely lagging in accepting new
  information (Frankfurter 2007).

2.2. Empirical Studies

During recent decades, the EMH has been widely analyzed on stock markets – qualitatively as well as quantitatively – following the objective of being able to draw a conclusion whether or not the EMH is present. Particularly the quantitative empirical studies have had the objective of determining which form of information efficiency goes along with stock price movements, in reality.

With reference to the qualitative arguments against the EMH, the joint-hypothesis-problem (Kosfeld 1996) as well as the information-paradox (Sommer 1999) must be mentioned.

The joint-hypothesis problem was recognized by Fama and describes the problem that (1991, p.1575): "Market efficiency per se is not testable. It must be tested jointly with some model of equilibrium, an asset pricing model. As a result, when we find anomalous evidence on the behavior of returns, the way it should be split between market inefficiency or a bad model of market equilibrium is ambiguous."

The information paradox introduced by Grossmann/Stiglitz (1980) state that – unlike the EMH – the information-generating process creates real costs. Due to the fact that actual stock market prices reflect all available information within an information-efficient market, nobody would be willing to make an effort to receive costly information. That wouldn't result in any advantages in comparison to simply using the actual stock market price. Yet, if all investors behave that way, the stock market would no longer be efficient, due to the fact that the information generating process – as an essential requirement for an efficient market – would no longer exist (Spremann 2006). Therefore, Grossmann/Stiglitz assume that markets have to be information-efficient to an extent to which costs – caused by the information generating process and the following evaluation of that information – have to at least be covered (Lo and MacKinlay 1999).

Concerning the quantitative analysis of the EMH, the empirical studies refer to the respective information efficiency form (Section 2.1.2.). The most important analysis tools and their respective analysis results are listed in the following:

- Weak form of information efficiency:
  The existence of the weak form of information efficiency can be tested by analyzing the predictability of future stock returns on the basis of historical stock prices (Hruby 1991).

Only if historical stock prices do not show any stochastic independence (i.e. correlation of zero) with future stock prices, can the weak form of information efficiency be assumed to exist. Otherwise the random walk characteristic of future stock prices cannot be considered as fulfilled.

On the one hand, the independence can be analyzed by autocorrelation, spectral and run tests, on the other hand, by filter techniques (Hoffmann 2001). Particularly the autocorrelation, spectral and run tests over the last thirty years have shown that historical stock prices are at least weakly correlated with future stock prices (Sapusek 1998).[1]

The empirical results of filter technique concepts – which analyze if mechanically triggered trading strategies are able to beat a simple buy-and-hold strategy – support the assumption that the random walk characteristic cannot be assumed to be existent on the stock market (Dressendörfer 1999).[2]

- Semi-strong form of information efficiency:

  The existence of the semi-strong form of information efficiency is tested by event studies, which analyze if actual stock market prices react immediately to new information (Sapusek 1998).

  The event studies prove that stock prices react to new information, but those reactions can take place biased and late (Shleifer 2000). Therefore, stock prices mostly reflect new information, but do not always "adjust rapidly and unbiased to new information", like Gonedes (1976, p.612) defined the

---

[1] Autocorrelation and run tests on the German stock market (1961-1972) show that the random walk hypothesis cannot be applied to the German stock market (Reiß 1974).
Autocorrelation and spectral tests on chosen stock indices prove the random walk hypothesis to be incorrect (Granger and Morgenstern 1970).
Autocorrelation tests on the New York Stock Exchange reject the random walk hypothesis (Kinney and Rozeff 1976) and the assumption of normal distribution (Fiellitz and Greene 1977).
[2] Alexander (1961 and 1964) proves the superiority of filter techniques in comparison to a simple buy-and-hold strategy, using the example of the Dow Jones and Standard and Poor's.
Blume and Fama (1966) criticize Alexander's results and show them to be wrong, if transaction costs are considered.
Filter techniques on the Austrian stock market (1965-1974) prove that historical stock prices and future stock prices are dependent and correlated (Uhlir 1979).
Bertoneche (1979) analyzes six European stock markets and draws the conclusion, that the application of filter techniques is able to beat a simple buy-and-hold strategy.

efficiency criteria of "fully reflected" by Fama (1970, p.383). Thus, the semi-strong form of information-efficiency cannot be confirmed in general.[3]

- Strong form of information efficiency:
  The existence of the strong form of information efficiency is tested by analyzing if insiders are able to generate an excess return on the stock market by using non-public information (Sapusek 1998). Empirical studies have shown that private information enables insiders to generate an excess return in comparison to investors who do not have access to that private information (Mörsch 2005). If that would not be the case, laws for generating transparency in terms of insider deals – like the German § 15a WpHG – would not be necessary (Spremann 2006). Science agrees that the strong form of information efficiency is not existent in reality (Mörsch 2005).[4]

2.3 Preliminary Conclusion

Under consideration of the controversial results of the empirical studies, it can be summarized that the EMH can be neither fully rejected nor can it be fully confirmed (Hruby 1991). Thus, stock analysis concepts like technical analysis, fundamental analysis and behavioral finance cannot generally be considered worthless (Dressendörfer 1998).

The joint-hypothesis-problem and particularly the theory of information paradox support the idea that these analysis concepts are necessary to achieve at least a certain level of information efficiency on the stock market (Albrecht and Maurer 2005).

So, which of the three efficiency forms exists on the stock market?

---

[3] Waud (1970) confirms the semi-efficient form by analyzing the effect of interest rate changes on the stock market.
Fama (1991) and Möller (1985) consider the semi-strong form of information efficiency to be proven by event studies on the German stock market.
Berry and Howe (1994) show that stock market prices react in a biased and late manner to new fundamental information.
[4] Meulbroek (1992) draws the conclusion that insiders are able to generate an excess return on the American stock market. Schmidt and Wulff (1993) confirm Meulbroek's statement for the German stock market.

At least the science seems to agree on the rejection of the strong form of information efficiency, because insiders are proven to be able to generate an excess return by using their private information.

With regard to the semi-strong form of information efficiency, science agrees that in general, stock prices react to new public information, but it is possible that these reactions can take place in a biased and late manner. That leads us to the conclusion that the semi-strong form generally cannot be confirmed over time.

The existence of the weak form of information efficiency is also doubtful, due to the fact that empirical studies have shown that the random walk characteristic of stock prices can be denied by autocorrelation, spectral and run tests. In addition to that, filter-techniques underline that mechanically triggered trading strategies seem to be at least temporarily able to generate an excess return, in comparison to simple buy-and-hold strategies.

With reference to an experimental study by Huber et al. (2006), the conclusion as to which of the three information efficiency forms is present on the stock market, cannot be given a general, final judgment, but rather is also dependent on the respective stock market cycle. This is due to the fact that influencing factors on information efficiency– like psychological factors and the application frequency of different analysis concepts – change over time with different stock market cycles (Shleifer 2000).

3. Fundamental Analysis

3.1. Definition and Premises

The term "fundamental analysis" is widely used in capital market analysis and therefore describes a wide range of fundamentally-driven analysis concepts (Cesar 1996). In the following, the term "fundamental analysis" encompasses the most important fundamentally-driven analysis concepts for determining the value of a company – expressed by the price of its stocks (Gantenbein and Spremann 2005).

Fundamental analysis is based on the premise that the actual stock market price fluctuates around its intrinsic value over time (Brigham and Houston 1998).

The intrinsic value is defined as the fair value of a company's stock. It is determined by analyzing which and to which extent fundamental factors have an influence on a company's value (Beike and Schlütz 2005, Mattern 2005). Finally, fundamentally-driven concepts – no matter which concept is considered – all have the same objective: comparing the calculated intrinsic value with the actual stock market price to be able to draw a conclusion, if the analyzed stock is undervalued or overvalued (Brigham and Houston 1998).

On the one hand, a stock is assumed to be undervalued if the intrinsic value lies under the actual stock market price (McLeavy and Solnik 2003). On the other hand, a stock is respectively assumed to be overvalued if the actual stock market price exceeds the intrinsic value of the stock (McLeavy and Solnik 2003).

The concept of intrinsic value implies that market participants are assumed to be rational in terms of buying a company's stock, because of the fundamental value of that company (Mattern 2005).

Nevertheless, fundamental analysis as a whole depends on the assumption that actual stock market prices do not always correctly reflect the real fundamental strength of a company. This is due to the fact that actual stock prices are also influenced by temporarily occurring anomalies, resulting in divergences between the intrinsic value and the actual stock market price in the short run (Franke and Hax 2003).

Those temporarily occurring anomalies are necessary for the successful application of fundamentally-driven analysis concepts. Otherwise, fundamental analysis would not be able to generate any advantage by determining the intrinsic value, because if at least a semi-efficient stock market is to be assumed – implying that actual stock market prices adjust rapidly and unbiased to new public fundamental information (Gonedes 1976) – the actual stock market price would already be equal to the intrinsic value of a stock. Therefore, fundamental analysis assumes that the market price of a stock ultimately follows its intrinsic value, but can vary from its intrinsic value in the short run (Bohl and Siklos 2001, Shiller 1981).

The fundamental value of a company – expressed by its intrinsic value – can be measured differently, leading to different fundamentally-driven analysis concepts that are explained in the following (Section 3.2.).

3.2. Company Evaluation Methods

With regard to the different premises of the most important value drivers as well as different motives for evaluating a company (Borowicz 2005), fundamentally-driven analysis methods are differentiated by different methods and approaches, shown in Figure 1:

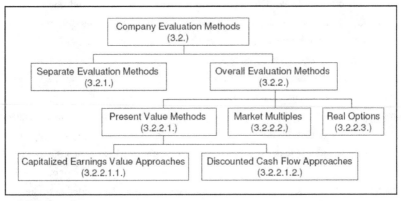

Figure 1: Overview of the Different Company Evaluation Methods (Coenenberg and Schultze 2002)

Depending on whether a company is considered by its separate assets and debts or as an interdependent complex, the analysis methods are subdivided into separate evaluation and overall evaluation methods (Dehmel and Hommel 2008). Due to its higher frequency of application and importance in practice (Gantenbein and Gehrig 2007), the following explanations of the basics as well as the most important advantages and disadvantages of the respective analysis methods are focused on the overall evaluation methods.

The overall evaluation methods are subdivided into present value methods, market multiples and real options, due to its different premises of how to evaluate a company fundamentally. With regard to its higher practical (Gantenbein and Gehrig 2007) and scientific (Prokop and Zimmermann 2002) relevance, the present value methods will be explained and discussed in detail and therefore, be subdivided into capitalized earnings value and discounted cash flow approaches.

3.2.1. Separate Evaluation Methods

The separate evaluation methods assume that the value of a company can be calculated by summing up the separately evaluated assets (a), subtracted by the nominal sum of debts (d) of the company (Deter et al. 2005a). Thus, the enterprise value (ev) can generally be expressed by the formula: $ev = a - d$.

The two most important separate evaluation methods are the net asset value approach and the liquidation value approach. They differ in terms of their respective going-concern premises (Drukarcyk and Schüler 2007). The net asset value approach assumes the continuation of the company, whereas the liquidation approach implies the liquidation of the company (Dehmel and Hommel 2008).

The net asset value of a company reflects the amount which would have been paid if a company had been identically reproduced (Brösel and Matschke 2007). It is calculated by summing up all operationally necessary assets of a company by its reproduction prices and then subtracting the sum of all debts by its nominal values. The result is added to the value of the sum of the entire operationally non-necessary assets of the company by its liquidation prices (Deter et al. 2005a).

The net asset value approach can be differentiated by two different concepts – the partial reproduction and the overall reproduction approach. The partial reproduction approach is limited on the evaluation of tangible assets, whereas the overall reproduction approach also takes estimated values for intangible assets into consideration (Dehmel and Homel 2008).

The liquidation value approach is applied in case of restructuring or termination of a company. It is calculated by summing up the company's assets according to its liquidation prices and subtracting the sum of debts by it respective nominal prices afterwards. The result has to be settled with the costs caused by the liquidation process of the assets. (Deter et al. 2005a).

Within the main context of fundamentally-driven analysis concepts, the net asset value approach, as well as the liquidation value approach, currently has the function of checking up the plausibility of values, calculated by overall evaluation methods (Kames 1999). Therefore, it fulfills the function of a lower value limit (Helbling 2007) or a value of correction (Dehmel and Homel 2008).

Unlike the overall valuation methods, the separate valuation methods just evaluate the actual value of a company's assets. That goes along with the disadvantage of ignoring future cash flows, generated by the interaction of different assets (Deter at al. 2005a). In addition to that, the evaluation of intangible assets is difficult and imprecise if reproduction or liquidation prices are used. Therefore, the separate valuation methods are currently mainly used either for companies, whose business is predominantly based on tangible assets, or to check up on whether the results of the overall valuation methods are plausible by delivering a lower value limit for the price paid for a company (Kames 1999).

3.2.2. Overall Evaluation Methods

Unlike the separate evaluation methods, the overall evaluation methods evaluate a company as a whole, by taking the interdependencies between separate assets and debts into consideration (Borowicz 2005). Therefore, "overall evaluation" means that assets and debts are evaluated in context, due to the fact that the company is evaluated as a whole (Ballwieser 2007). The overall evaluation methods can be subdivided into present value methods (Section 3.2.2.1.), market multiples (Section 3.2.2.2.) and real options (Section 3.2.2.3.), which are explained in the following.

3.2.2.1. Present Value Methods

Present value methods are based on the premises of the future-oriented capital budgeting approach (Deter et al. 2005a, Drukarczyk and Schüler 2007). This leads to the conclusion that the value of a company is represented by the present value of all net-incomes of the investor (De Fusco et al. 2001, Helbling 2001).

Depending on how these net-incomes are defined, present value methods are subdivided into earnings and cash flow approaches (Beike and Schlütz 2005). Therefore, a differentiation must be maintained between the capitalized earnings value and discounted cash flow approaches (Borowicz 2005).

In terms of the structure of the method for calculating the respective income figure, it doesn't matter whether earnings or cash-flows are calculated. In both approaches, the evaluation period is subdivided into two time periods – t and n (Borowicz 2005, Streitferdt 2008).

The first period extends over a time period of three to five years (t) (Streitferdt 2008) and calculates the income on the basis of the companies business plans (Borowicz 2005) or a concrete estimation of the respective evaluator (Henselmann 2002). The second period encompasses the subsequent years up to eternity (n) (Streitferdt 2008) and calculates a residual income, which is calculated by deriving steadily achievable values of the first evaluation period and extrapolating those to eternity (Henselmann 2002).

In addition to different income figures, the two approaches also differ in terms of their discounting factors (Borowicz 2005). The discounting factor of the earnings approach is calculated by adding an estimated risk premium to a risk free rate, whereas the discounting factors of the cash-flow approaches vary from the expected return of shareholders (equity-approach) to the expected return of shareholders as well as creditors (entity-approach) (Bruns and Steiner 2007, Hachmeister 1994).

In comparison to other fundamentally-driven analysis concepts – such as overall evaluation methods and market multiples – the present value methods have the advantage of taking the time value of money explicitly into consideration (Dehmel and Hommel 2008). In addition to that, the consideration of earnings or cash flows better reflects the interdependent value of a company than the overall evaluation methods (Deter et al. 2005a) and is less susceptible to market-driven misinterpretations, like the approach of market multiples (Damodaran 2006).

With regard to the disadvantages of the present value approaches, one can argue that particularly the residual value of a company is often characterized by uncertainty, yet has a share in overall value of the company from approximately 50 to 80 percent (Henselmann 2002, Hoke 2002).

In the following, the capitalized earnings value approach as well as the different discounted cash flow approaches are explained and evaluated in terms of their advantages and disadvantages.

3.2.2.1.1. Capitalized Earnings Value Approaches

Capitalized earnings value approaches calculate the value of a company by discounting and capitalizing the future sustainable earnings of a company (Borowicz 2005). Moxter (1994) defines the capitalized earnings value as the sum of financial and non-financial values of a company.

With regard to their practical application, the reference figure for describing the sustainable success of a company can vary, depending on the preferences of the evaluator. On the one hand, balance sheet-driven success figures like EBT can be used (Borowicz 2005). On the other hand, the application of adjusted and more cash-flow oriented success figures, such as EBIT and EBITDA, are also possible (Deter et al. 2005a).

The discounting factor is based on the idea of an alternative comparable investment opportunity (Deter et al. 2005a) and reflects the costs of equity (Dehmel and Hommel 2007). The costs of equity are calculated by two steps:

In the first step, a risk free rate of return is determined – usually by considering the return of a risk-free rate, such as a triple A-rated government bond (Borowicz 2005).

In a second step, a risk premium is added for meeting the requirement of considering individual risk drivers, like operative, capital structure and industry sector risk factors (Borowicz 2005).

In comparison with the discounted cash flow approaches, the capitalized earnings approach has two disadvantages:

The capitalized earnings approach falls back on an imprecisely defined discounting factor, which can lead to different results in practice, due to the respective definition of the applied discounting factor (Deter et al. 2005a, Dehmel and Hommel 2008).

Also, balance sheet-driven success figures are more susceptible to manipulations than cash-flow oriented figures (Behringer 2007, Deter et al 2005a).

According to Borowicz (2005), as well as Drukarczyk and Schüler (2007), the capitalized earnings value approach can be considered as the German version of the DCF equity approach, due to its similarities.

3.2.2.1.2. Discounted Cash Flow Approaches

Discounted cash flow approaches calculate the value of a company by discounting its future cash flows (Borowicz 2005). The discounted cash flow approach is differentiated by three methods: weighted average cost of capital (WACC), adjusted present value, and the equity methods:

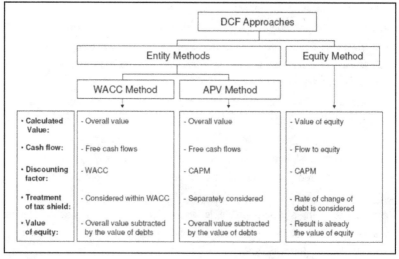

Figure 2: Systematization of the Discounted Cash Flow Approaches (Steiner and Bruns 2007)

Figure 2 illustrates that the three methods differ in terms of the definition of their cash flows and their different discounting factor, which has influence on the treatment of the company's tax shield (Bruns and Steiner 2007), explained in the following:

- WACC method:

  Formula: $\sum_{t=1}^{n} \dfrac{FCF_t}{(1+i_{WACC})^t} + \dfrac{RV_n}{(1+i_{WACC})^n} - debts$.

  The WACC method is based on the assumption that the company is first evaluated under the point of view of all providers of capital – equity as well as debts (Bruns and Steiner 2007). Therefore, the cash flow is expressed by the

Free Cash Flow (FCF), which still contains the cash flows obtained by creditors (Deter et al. 2005b).

The free cash flows are discounted by the WACC, which expresses the expected return of shareholders as well as creditors (Copeland et al. 2002, Vettiger and Volkart 2002). The WACC is calculated by the formula:

$$WACC = i_{CAPM} * \frac{E}{TC} + (i_d * (1 - tr)) * \frac{D}{TC}.$$

The expected return of the shareholders (i_{CAPM}) as well as the expected return of the creditors, multiplied by the company's tax shield $(i_d * (1 - tr))$, is respectively weighted with the ratio of equity and total capital $\left(\frac{E}{TC}\right)$, or debt $\left(\frac{D}{TC}\right)$, and total capital (Behringer 2007).

In a second step, the residual value of the company (RV) is also discounted by the WACC.

The sum of WACC-discounted free cash flows and residual value expresses the value of the company under the point of view of both, the shareholders and the creditors. Therefore, the value of debts has to be subtracted afterwards to ensure that the value of equity of the company remains (Deter et al. 2005).

- APV method:

  Formula: $\sum\limits_{t=1}^{n} \frac{FCF_t}{(1 + i_{CAPM})^t} + \frac{RV_n}{(1 + i_{CAPM})^n} + \sum\limits_{t=1}^{n} \frac{i_d * d_t * tr}{(1 + i_d)^t} - debts$.

The APV can be considered as the modified version of the WACC, dividing the value of the company into its separate value drivers (Drukarczyk and Schüler 2007, Krolle 2001).

In the first step, the company is assumed to be fully self-financed, so that the operative value of the company can be considered separately from the value of the company's capital structure (Deter et al. 2005, Krolle 2001). Therefore, the free cash flows are not discounted by the WACC, but only by the expected return of the shareholders (i_{CAPM}). Analogous thereto is that the residual value of the company is also discounted by the shareholders' expected return (Vettiger and Volkart 2002).

In a second step, the value of the tax shield is calculated by the sum of the interest rate for debts (i_d), the amount of debts (d_t) and the company's tax rate (tr), discounted by the interest rate for debts.

In order to achieve the value of equity, the sum of CAPM-discounted free cash flows and residual value, as well as the value of the tax shield, are subtracted by the value of debts at the end.

In comparison to the WACC method, the APV has the advantage of generating transparency in terms of the respective value drivers of the company (Steiner and Wallmeier 1999).

- Equity method:

  Formula: $\displaystyle\sum_{t=1}^{n} \frac{FTE_t}{(1+i_{CAPM})^t} + \frac{RV_n}{(1+i_{CAPM})^n}$.

In contrast to the entity methods, the equity method only considers the cash flows obtained by the shareholders – the so called Flows to Equity (FTE) (Damodaran 2002, Deter et al. 2005).

In analogy to the applied cash flow definition, the flows to equity are only discounted by the expected return of the shareholders (i_{CAPM}) in a first step. In a second step, the residual value of the company (RV) is determined and also discounted by the expected return of the shareholders (Vettiger and Volkart 2002).

The sum of CAPM-discounted flows to equity and residual value already reflects the company's value of equity. Unlike the WACC and APC methods, the equity method already considers the debts of the company in its cash flow definition, such that the distraction of debts at the end is omitted (Drukarczyk and Schüler 2007).

With regards to the advantages and disadvantages of the discounted cash flow concept as a whole, the following conclusions can be determined:

Unlike balance-sheet driven success figures, cash-flows are less susceptible to manipulations (Behringer 2007, Deter et al 2005a). This explains its superiority in comparison to its most similar evaluation method – the capitalized earnings value approach. On the other hand, the estimation of future cash flows can be complex in practice, due to the large number of influencing factors on the estimated cash flow (Damodaran 2001).

The application of the CAPM has the advantage of a consistent structure for determining the shareholders expected return (Hachmeister 1994), but goes along with the disadvantages of the CAPM (Müller and Röder 2001, Vettiger and Volkart 2002), as well as its complex application in practice, e.g. the application of consistently determined betas by different evaluators (Ballwieser 1995, Damodaran 2001).

Nevertheless, the discounted cash flow methods have been established as the most frequently used analysis methods in practice (Bömelburg et al. 1994, Hillers et al. 1999), which supports their advantages in comparison to other fundamentally-driven analysis concepts.

3.2.2.2. Market Multiples

The application of market multiples is based on the premise, that the value of a company can be derived by comparing a predefined performance figure of the evaluated company with the value of that performance figure of a comparable company (Coenenberg and Schultze 2002).

Therefore, the formula for calculating the fair value of the evaluated company is described by (Demmel and Hommel 2008): $p(e) = f_e * \dfrac{p(c)}{f_c} = f_e * m_i$.

Whereby:

$p(e)$ = searched price of the evaluated company

f_e = performance figure of the evaluated company

$p(c)$ = kwon price of the comparable company

f_c = performance figure of the comparable company

m_i = multiple.

The multiple can refer to profit-orientated, earnings-orientated (e.g. EBITDA, EBIT), cash-flow-orientated (sales, cash-flows) or other-oriented (customers, visitors) parameters, that are adequate to measure the value of the company (Bruns and Steiner 2007, Seppelfricke 1999).

The multiple is determined by the comparative company approach, which is differentiated by its three sub-methods, differing in terms of its derivation methods of the multiple:

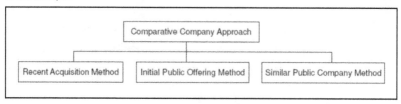

Figure 3: The Three Methods of the Comparative Company Approach (Dehmel and Homel 2008)

The recent acquisition method derives the multiple from recently executed transactions, whereas the initial public offering approach calculates the multiple based on recently paid prices for companies that have gone public (Dehmel and Hommel 2008). In contrast to that, the similar public company method takes each comparable publicly-quoted company into consideration (Bausch 2000).

If its possible, the respective multiple is not only derived by taking a single comparable company into consideration, but by building a peer group that is as similar as possible to the evaluated company in terms of its industry sector, growth rate and risk structure (Drukarczyk and Schüler 2007). Otherwise, the expressiveness of the used multiple has to be severely challenged.

In addition to that, there are some other arguments that put the concept of multiples into question: The market price of the company's peer group builds the basis for evaluating the considered company. That could lead to a misinterpretation of the company's real value, if the entire peer group is wrongly priced by the stock market (Fleischer 1999). In hindsight, this was the case during the new economy phase at the end of the 20th century (Perkins and Perkins 1999), where the heavy use of market multiples at least supported the process of wrong stock pricing (Hoffmann 2001), due to the fact that the peer group itself was wrongly priced by the market. Furthermore, multiples belong to the group of static analysis concepts, meaning that future growth rates are not taken into consideration (Deter et al. 2005a). That could have a serious impact on the comparability of companies if the considered companies clearly differ in their predicted future growth rates (Dehmel and Hommel 2008).

Taking these aspects into consideration, the IDW (2007) advises that the concept of multiples should only be used for checking the plausibility of results of other more detailed and dynamic concepts, such as the discounted cash flow or the capitalized earnings value approach (Aders et al. 2000, Auge-Dickhut and Moser 2003).

Nevertheless, Kames' (1999) examinations of the application frequency of multiples – which proved that 72% of all financial analysts always use the concept of multiples when a company has to be evaluated – indicates that the concept of multiples has its advantages. This is particularly due to the fact that multiples are persuasive in terms of a simple, fast and inexpensive application for determining at least a broad price range for a potentially fair value of a company (Deter et al. 2005a, Krolle et al. 2005, Stock 2001).

3.2.2.3. Real Options

The concept of real options is based on the premise that management's flexibility to react to modified circumstances has a value itself, which should be taken into consideration when a company is evaluated (Crasselt and Tomaszewski 1999). Brown and Reilly (2006, p.979) are convinced that "conventional net present value calculations ignore the benefits of flexibility and may therefore undervalue projects that allow companies to react rapidly to changing circumstances."

This is due to the assumption of present value concepts, which states that actions by the company's management are not flexible but static (Antikarov et al. 2003). This leads to the conclusion that present value concepts are based on the assumption of a symmetrically distributed future company value, whereas the concept of real options is based on an asymmetrical distribution assumption (Allen et al. 2006). Unlike real options, present value concepts therefore underestimate the value of a company (Antikarov et al 2003).

On the basis of the concept of financial options, the flexibility of the management's decisions is measured by real options – e.g. options to expand, options to abandon, timing options, production options etc. (Allen et al. 2006, Deter et al. 2005a). Those real options always have a value, so that the value of a company is composed by a static value – analogous to the present value concepts – and the sum of the options' values (Antikarov et al. 2003).

With regard to its practical applicability, the concept of real options is subjected to the following restrictions:

Firstly, the underlying of the real option is usually not traded on an organized market (Kasperzak and Krag 2007), which also means that the volatility of the underlying option is a non-observable stochastic parameter (Beckmann et al. 2002, Hommel and Pritsch 1999). Unlike the concept of financial options, those uncertainties about the correct value of parameters for calculating the fair value of a real option (Dück-Rath 2005) leads to biased and uncertain results (Brown and Reily 2006, Damodaran 2001).

Secondly, the estimation as well as the following transfer of the future flexibilities of the managements' decisions into real options is difficult to execute for external observers such as financial analysts (Deter et al. 2005a).

Due to its uncertainties and its difficulties of an adequate practicability in practice (Beckmann et al. 2002) as well as its price-raising characteristic, the concept of real option is mostly recommended as an addition to present value methods, being able to check the plausibility of its results and building an upper limit for the value of a company (Damodaran 2006, Deter et al. 2005a).

3.3. Empirical Studies

The following empirical studies examine the importance and the evidence of fundamental analysis in the stock market as well as the relevance and usefulness of its respective analyzing methods.

A number of empirical studies that deliberate over the question as to whether or not stock prices fluctuate around their intrinsic value have been conducted. Therefore, the empirical studies examine the relationship between figures expressing the fundamental strength of a company – e.g. the dividend rate, price earnings ratio (PEG) and price book ratio (PBR) – and its real stock price development over time.

The majority of empirical studies come to the conclusion that stock prices follow their intrinsic value.[6]

On the other hand, there are some other empirical studies that have proven that stock price developments cannot completely be explained by fundamental factors. This is due to the impact of non-fundamental influencing factors on the stock price.[7]

Putting these two aspects together, we can draw the conclusion that the most important premise of fundamental analysis – stock prices follow its intrinsic value in the long run but can diverge form its intrinsic value in the short run – can be seen as empirically proven.

In a second step, the relevance and the usefulness of the explained fundamentally-driven analysis concepts is examined by Gantenbein and Gehrig (2007). The examination extends over all important evaluators – publicly quoted companies, financial analysts, consultancies and auditors – who participate in the stock market.

---

[6] Easton (1985) as well as Sorensen and Williamson (1985) examine the relationship between future expected dividends and real stock price movement on the American stock market by a regression model and come to the conclusion that there is an empirical relationship between those two figures.
Ou and Penman (1993) proved a significantly positive autocorrelation between the return on equity (ROE) and the stock price of a company in the American stock market during the considered period from 1969 to 1985.
Fairfield (1994) proved a significantly positive autocorrelation between price earnings ratios (PER) or price book ratios (PBR) and the stock price of a company in the American stock market during the considered period from 1970 to 1984.
De Bondt and Thaler (1987) and Lakonishok et al. (1994) state that, historically, portfolios of companies with low PBR barely earned higher returns than those with high PBR.
[7] Binswanger (2004) examines the relationship between fundamental influencing factors on stock price shocks by applying a bivariate SVAR model, which includes growth rates of industrial production and stock prices. Considering a period from 1960 to 1999, Biswanger comes to the conclusion that "real activity shocks only explain a small fraction of the variability in real stock prices in the US, Japan and an aggregate European economy since the early 1980s, while they explain a substantial portion over the 1960s and 1970s in all area" (p. 185). Chung and Lee's (1998) as well as Lee's (1995, 1998) examinations arrive at comparable results.

Table 1 shows the results of the examination:

		Criteria	
		Relevance	Usefulness
Analysis Approaches	Separate Evaluation Methods	2,85	2,95
	Capitalized Earnings Value Approaches	3,76	3,72
	Dicounted Cash Flow Approaches	4,17	4,07
	Market Multiples	3,92	3,90
	Real Options	2,36	2,52

Table 1: Evaluation of the Relevance and Usefulness of the Different Fundamental Analysis Approaches (Gantenbein and Gehrig 2007)

The respective score achieved by an analysis approach is calculated by the arithmetical average of all evaluators. Five points are the highest score that can be achieved by an analysis approach. The higher the score achieved by an analysis approach, the more relevant respectively useful the analysis approach.

With regard to the result, it can be stated that overall evaluation methods are judged to be more important and useful than the separate evaluation methods.

Within the overall evaluation methods, the DCF approaches and the market multiples are considered to be the most relevant and useful methods.

Real options are judged to be less relevant and useful, whereas capitalized earnings value approaches are considered to be less important than the similar concepts of DCF.

Summing up those results, we can conclude that discounted cash flow approaches and market multiples are considered to be the most relevant and useful fundamentally-driven analysis methods in practice. This is backed up by the fact that the majority of evaluators use a combination of discounted cash flow and market multiples in practice, in order to combine their respective strengths (Aders et al. 2000, Dehmel and Hommel 2008, Gantenbein and Gehrig 2007).

3.4. SWOT Analysis

In the following, the respective strengths, weaknesses, opportunities and threats of the concept of fundamental analysis are explained:

- Strengths:
  - By comparing the theoretically justified intrinsic values of stock with the actual stock market prices, we can conclude how far actual stock market prices reflect fundamentally justified values.
  - Present value methods consider the respective value drivers of a company, enabling the evaluator to gain an impression about which fundamental factors will have influence on the company's development in the future.
  - The company's value drivers are represented in models, so that we can argue why the fair value of a company achieves a certain amount.

- Weaknesses:
  - Fundamental analysis is able to judge whether a stock is undervalued or overvalued within a considered future time period of normally three to six months, but it is not appropriate for giving an advice at which point in time the evaluated stock should be bought or sold.
  - Fundamentally-driven investors only succeed in buying or selling undervalued respectively overvalued stocks, if the market discovers the undervaluation or overvaluation of the stock, so that the gap between stock market prices and intrinsic value are diminished over time.
  However, phases of undervaluation or overvaluation can go on for time periods that clearly exceed the fundamentally predicted time period of three to six months, so that the fundamentally-driven concepts are not appropriate in indicating when the majority of market participants can be expected to discover the undervaluation or overvaluation of a company.
  - The concept of fundamental analysis assumes the majority of market participants to be rational in terms of evaluating a company by its fundamental strengths. In phases of crash and boom, the impact of fundamental information is weakening, whereas psychological factors are gaining in importance, such that the basic assumption of rational market participants is temporarily overruled.

- Empirical studies have shown that fundamentally-driven evaluators are not only influenced by fundamental information, but also by irrationalities – particularly during extreme phases – so that the determination of the intrinsic value gets biased by those irrationalities (Mattern 2005).

- Opportunities:
  - The concept of fundamental analysis could be supplemented by evaluation approaches that have its strengths in terms of giving a timing advice, at which point in time an undervalued or overvalued stock should be bought or sold.
  - Due to the fact that irrational behavior particularly gains in impact during extreme market phases (Florek 2000), the concept of fundamental analysis could be supplemented by evaluation approaches that are not based on the assumption of rationally but irrationally behaving market participants.
  - Fundamentally-driven stock market evaluators could be professionally coached in behavioral finance, aimed at the objective to become aware of the factors that drive evaluators to behave irrationally – particularly during extreme market phases. With regard to their function as information intermediates, irrational cascade effects, extending to further stock market participants (Bikhchandani et al. 1998), could partially be prevented.

- Threats:
  - Assuming that stock markets can be proven to be permanently at least semi-efficient, the concept of fundamental analysis would not be able to generate advantages for stock market investors any longer.
  - If fundamentally-driven stock market evaluators turn out to be subjected by irrationalities on their own, the calculation of fundamentally justified fair values is doubtful.

3.5. Preliminary Conclusion

Empirical studies have proven that actual stock market prices follow company's intrinsic values in the long run, but can diverge in the short run, because of non-fundamental influencing factors. Therefore the main premises of fundamental analysis – stock prices fluctuating around intrinsic values – can be assumed to be confirmed empirically.

By determining the intrinsic value of a company and comparing the received value with the actual stock market price, fundamental analysis is able to draw a conclusion as to whether a stock should be bought or sold.

The determination of a company's intrinsic value can be established by applying different fundamentally-driven analysis concepts that are differentiated by separate or overall evaluation methods. With regard to their scientific as well as practical relevance and usefulness, the separate evaluation methods are negligible, whereas the overall evaluation methods are preferred. Particularly DCF methods and capitalized earnings value approaches as well as market multiples are heavily applied for determining the company's intrinsic value.

Considering the concept of fundamental analysis as a whole, we can draw the conclusion that fundamental analyses not only enable evaluators to determine whether actual stock market prices are fundamentally justified, but rather also enable evaluators to gain an impression by which and to which extent companies' intrinsic values are affected by different influencing factors.

Nevertheless, the concept of fundamental analysis also has its weaknesses. It is not possible to state a precise point in time when a stock should be bought or sold, but rather only a space of time during which a stock is undervalued or overvalued. It isn't also possible to predict or explain non-fundamentally-driven stock price movements, due to assumptions of rationally acting market participants.

Taking these aspects into consideration, fundamental analysis is an important concept for being able to evaluate company's stock prices, but can be improved in terms of concrete timing decisions as well as considering non-rational influencing factors.

4. Behavioral Finance

4.1. Definition and Premises

"At the most general level, behavioral finance is the study of human fallibility in competitive markets." (Shleifer 2000, p.23) With regard to the stock market, behavioral finance examines psychological and sociological impacts on the stock market in order to explain stock market phenomena – so called anomalies (Oehler 2000, Schäffer and Vater 2002).

The term "anomaly" was created during the eighties by the advocates of the traditional finance theory, which considered stock market phenomena to be abnormal, due to the fact that those phenomena were not explainable by the prevailing capital market theories – e.g. EMH and CAPM (Frankfurter 2007, Lawrence et al. 2007, Montier 2007, Shefrin 2000).

In contrast to neoclassical capital market theories, behavioral finance does not assume the market participants to be rational but irrational (Avramov and Tarun 2006), due to naturally given human restrictions that prevent the market participants from behaving like a homo oeconomicus, e.g. in terms of restrictions during the information perception (Goldberg and von Nitzsch 2000, Miller 1956, Schäffer and Vater 2002).

Assuming that those irrationalities are inevitably made by each market participant – at least to the extent of unchangeable natural restrictions – failures are systematically made, such that anomalies become predictable (Behavioral Finance Group 1999). The behavioral finance approach can therefore be considered as an attempt to supplement the rationally-based capital market theories by psychological and sociological cognitions (Schäffer and Vater 2002).

The scientific acceptance of the behavioral finance approach was achieved at the beginning of the eighties and can be traced back to two circumstances:

On the one hand, empirical studies increasingly proved that capital market developments cannot be completely explained by the prevailing capital market theories (Lawrence et al. 2007, Shefrin 2000, Schäffer and Vater 2002). On the other hand, those practical observations were scientifically backed up by Kahneman and Tverskey's (1979) "prospect theory", which explained the investor's behavior by taking behavioral anomalies into consideration.

Nowadays, the prospect theory is considered to be the foundation of the behavioral finance approach (Shefrin 2002), due to the fact that it was the first scientific theory that proved the market participants to behave irrationally (Frankfurter 2007).

Nevertheless, behavioral finance is not a closed theory but consists of a number of separate theories that can, firstly, be categorized by the considered aggregation level (Schäffer and Vater 2002) and, secondly, along the market participants' investment process.

4.2. Anomalies

The concept of behavioral finance can be subdivided in terms of the considered aggregation level (Schäffer and Vater 2002). Based on the examination of the market participants' individual behavior, anomalies can be aggregated to a higher consideration level.

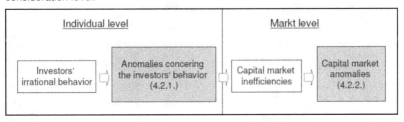

Figure 4: Anomalies Concerning the Investors' Behavior and Capital Market Anomalies

Figure 4 illustrates that observable capital market anomalies are the result of capital market inefficiencies. These capital market inefficiencies are caused by anomalies concerning the investors' behavior, which are just the observable consequences of investors' irrational behavior. The respective anomalies concerning the investors' behavior (Section 4.2.1.), as well as the derived capital market anomalies (Section 4.2.2.), are explained in the following chapters.

4.2.1. Anomalies Concerning the Investors Behavior

Anomalies concerning the investors' behavior can be categorized by the point in time of their occurrence during the investment process:

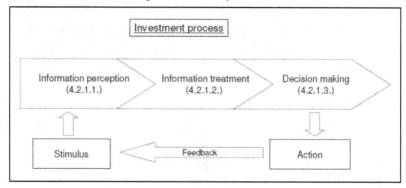

Figure 5: The Three Phases of the Investment Process

Figure 5 shows that the investment process consists of three consecutive levels – information perception (Section 4.2.1.1.), information treatment (Section 4.2.1.2.) and decision making (Section 4.2.1.3.) – where there can be anomalies concerning the investors' behavior. The final decision leads to the action of buying or not buying, or respectively, selling or not selling a stock. The respective action is connected with a feedback perceived as a stimulus by the investor. It triggers the restart of the investment process from its beginning.

The number of anomalies discovered by the behavioral finance approach exceeds the framework of this thesis, such that only the most important anomalies – measured by the importance of their impacts on the capital market - are explained in the following. In order to establish a structured presentation of the different theories, why investors behave irrationally, the various anomalies are differentiated by their point in time of occurrence during the investment process.

4.2.1.1. Information Perception

Examinations have shown that human beings are naturally restricted in terms of processing stimuli (Goldberg and von Nitzsch 2000, Kahneman and Tversky 2000). With regard to the stock market, the quantity of stimuli (e.g. new information) creates a complexity that exceeds the market participants' naturally given capabilities to correctly process those stimuli (Buskamp 2004).

In order to be able to reduce the given complexity, market participants are unconsciously or even consciously subjected by heuristics, which have the effect of reducing the given complexity, but which can also lead to a biased perception of information (Goldberg and von Nitzsch 2000, Shefrin 2002). Montier (2007) defines heuristics as rules of thumb that allow the investor to deal with informational deluge.

With regard to rationally-based finance theories, the heuristics are considered to be irrational, due to the fact that the concept of homo oeconomicus assumes human beings not to be subjected by naturally restrictions (Muth 1961, Dangel et al. 2001, De Bondt and Brav 2002). Therefore, heuristics lead to anomalies that cannot be explained by those rationally-based finance theories (Frankfurter 2007, Lawrence et al. 2007, Montier 2007, Shefrin 2000).

Figure 2 overviews the most important information perception anomalies with their respective definition:

Anomaly	Definition
Framing	The perception of information depends on the environmental circumstances (Shefrin 2002, Tversky 2004).
Selective perception	Information that confirms the previous expectation is preferred by investors (Kahneman and Tversky 2000).
Availability heuristics	Easily accessible information is overvalued (Andreassen 1990).
Adaptation of mass opinions	Opinions of opinion leaders and reference groups are perceived and adapted rather than those of other groups (Maas and Weibler 1997, Shiller 2000).

Table 2: Information Perception Anomalies

The concept of framing can be derived from Kahneman's and Tversky's prospect theory and assumes that the perception of information depends on environmental circumstances (Shefrin 2002, Tversky 2004). Therefore, the investors' perception is influenced by the way the information is presented (Laser 1995) – usually exploited by a company's investor relations unit in practice (Breuer 2008).

The concept of selective perception is based on the theory of cognitive dissonances[8] and assumes that investors prefer information that confirms their expectations in order to reduce dissonances (Bergold and Mayer 2005, Kahneman and Tversky 2000).

Availability heuristics expect investors to overvalue easily accessible information (Andreassen 1990), due to the fact that difficultly accessible information is connected with high costs and efforts, which are avoided by the investor (Goldberg and von Nitzsch 2000).

With regard to the perception and treatment of information, opinion leaders – e.g. famous analysts or stock gurus – as well as reference groups have an important impact on the investors' perception (Maas and Weibler 1997). Their opinions are rather perceived and adapted by investors than those of other information sources, because "people are respectful of authorities in formulating the opinions about which they will later be so overconfident, transferring their confidence in authorities to their own judgments based upon them." (Shiller 2000, p.151)

4.2.1.2. Information Treatment

With regard to the information treatment, investors are subjected by further heuristics in order to simplify complex subjects. These simplifications are necessary for being able to evaluate a subject, but also go along with the danger of a biased or wrong information treatment (Goldberg and von Nitzsch 2000, Kiehling 2001).

---

[8] The term "cognitive dissonance" expresses an emotional condition, where two cognitions (e.g. opinions, beliefs, and moral concepts of an investor) are not in line with each other (Beckmann 1984). Investors try to reduce those dissonances in order to be in harmony with themselves (Bergold and Mayer 2005).

Figure 3 overviews the most important information treatment anomalies with their respective definition:

Anomaly	Definition
Simplification	Complex circumstances are reduced to the seemingly most important facts (Goldberg and von Nitsch 2000, Kiehling 2001).
Reference point effect	Gains and losses are relatively judged to a reference point (Bergold and Mayer 2005, Herrmann et al. 2000, Kahneman and Tversky 2000, Odean 1998).
Loss aversion	Losses are sensed stronger than gains of the same amount (Kahneman and Tversky 2000, Odean 1998, Shefrin 2002).
Mental accounting	Economically identical events are differently judged, due to different evaluation criteria (Kahneman and Tversky 1981, Shefrin 2002).
Anchoring	Estimations are geared too strongly on previous data (Neale and Northcraft 1987, Shefrin 2002, Tvede 2002).
Information source effect	Same information from different sources enhances the belief of its correctness (Dreman 1998).
Representativeness	Judging circumstances by how they appear rather than how statistically likely they are (Montier 2007, Shefrin 2002).
Probability weighing	Wrong probability weighing of future events leads to a higher risk willingness of previous winners and a lower risk willingness of previous losers (Peterson 2007).
Reversal of risk willingness	Decreasing risk sensibility during long lasting trends can suddenly reverse (Jünemann and Schellenberger 1997).

Table 3: Information Treatment Anomalies

The reference point effect as well as the concept of loss aversion is based on the prospect theory, the value function of which is illustrated in Figure 6:

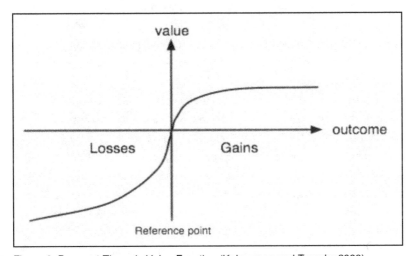

Figure 6: Prospect Theory's Value Function (Kahneman and Tversky 2000)

With regard to the development of the value function, we can draw the conclusion that investors do not just perceive relatively (Section 4.2.1.1.), but also evaluate in a relative manner (Goldberg and von Nitzsch 2000). The stock purchase price serves as a reference point to the investor (Bergold and Mayer 2005, Herrmann et al. 2000). Gains as well as losses are relatively judged to this referent point (Kahneman and Tversky 2000, Odean 1998).

The concave (gain area) or convex (loss area) development of the value function shows, that the bigger the distance between the reference point and the actual stock price, the lower the investor's sensitivity towards these gains respectively losses (Kahneman and Tversky 2000).

Furthermore, another anomaly can be derived by considering the ascending slope of the value function – the so called investors' loss aversion (Kahneman and Tversky 2000, Odean 1998, Shefrin 2002). Within the loss area, the value function develops steeper than within the gain area, which leads to the conclusion that losses are sensed stronger by the investor than gains of the same amount (Kahneman and Tversky 2000).

The different treatment of gains and losses can partially be explained by the mental accounting phenomenon, which assumes the investor to have different mental accounts for evaluating investments (Kahneman and Tversky 1981, Shefrin 2002). Therefore, investors do not evaluate their portfolio as a whole, but by considering the success or failure of any investment on its own, in order to simplify the complexity of interdependencies between different investments (Goldberg and von Nitzsch 2000). With regard to the stock market, mental accounting prevents the investor from building a well diversified portfolio – one of the basic objectives of the modern portfolio theory.

The concept of anchoring is closely connected with the reference point effect and assumes that future estimations are geared too strongly on previous data (Neale and Northcraft 1987, Shefrin 2002, Tvede 2002), which is particularly a problem for evaluators' future predictions – particularly analysts (Amir and Ganzach 1998). Other important anomalies in terms of the information treatment – especially to be able to explain booms and crashes on the stock market (De Grauwe and Grimaldi 2004, Lawrence et al. 2007) – are the information source effect as well as the concepts of representativeness, probability weighing and the reversal of risk.

The information source effect assumes the investor to be more convinced by the correctness of information, the more that independent sources generate identical information (Dreman 1998). In addition to the concept of representativeness – considering investors to judge circumstances by how they appear rather than how likely they are statistically (Montier 2007, Shefrin 2002) – those two concepts lead to the wrong probability weighing of future events (Peterson 2007).

Therefore, successful investors assume previous events to be representative for the future. This expectation is supported by an increasingly one-sided information basis during a long lasting trend (Bertram and Hass 2008), leading to a decreasing risk sensibility. The investors are strongly used to the prevailing trend, so that a sudden trend reversal leads to strong reactions, due to the fact that investors were mentally unprepared to the changed situation (Jünemann and Schellenberger 1997).

4.2.1.3. Decision Making

Decision making anomalies are the result of afore mentioned anomalies during the phases of information perception and treatment. Figure 4 overviews the most important decision-making anomalies with their respective definition:

Anomaly	Definition
Illusion of control	Investors consider the future events on the stock market to be controllable (White 1959, Langer 1975).
Overconfidence	Investors estimate themselves to be better than the average of investors (Daniel et al. 2001, Henze et al. 2003, Laschke 1999, Shefrin 2002).
Home bias	Investors tend to overweight stocks from their homeland, due to the illusion of being able to evaluate those stocks better than stocks from foreign (French and Poterba 1991, Schiereck 2000).
Disposition effect	Gains are taken too early whereas losses are ridden to long (Heilamm et al. 2000, Kiehling 2008, Vossmann 1999).
Selective decision making	Mental attachment to previous made decisions leads to timely biased reactions for reversing those decisions (Goldberg and von Nitzsch 2000).
Regret avoidance	In case of doubt the investor does not sell his loss-generating stock, because the active confession of misjudgment causes a stronger discomfiture than passiveness (Bergold and Mayer 2005, Tvede 2002).

Table 4: Decision Making Anomalies

Illusion of control describes the phenomenon where market participants are subjected to the illusion that future events on the stock market can be controlled by them, although this is not the case in reality (White 1959, Langer 1975).

With regard to the predictability of future events, the illusion of control goes along with investors' overconfidence (Goldberg and von Nitzsch 2000). De Bondt and

Thaler (1995, p.393) are convinced that "overconfidence explains why portfolio managers trade so much, why pension funds hire active equity managers, and why even financial economists often hold actively managed portfolios – they all think they can pick the winners."

The home bias effect can be derived from the illusion of control as well as the overconfidence effect. Investors consider themselves to be able to evaluate domestic stocks better than stocks from abroad, resulting in overweighing domestic stocks (French and Poterba 1991). As a consequence of the home bias effect, investors do not diversify their portfolios optimally (Schiereck 2000), which represents a further breach of modern portfolio theory.

The disposition effect assumes the investor to be averse to risk within the gain area, but risk-seeking within the loss area, which leads to the conclusion that gains are taken too early, whereas losses are ridden to long (Heilmann et al. 2000, Kiehling 2008, Vossmann 1999).[9] The disposition effect is the aggregated result of the reference point as well as the loss aversion effect (see 4.2.1.2.) (Oehler 2000). Furthermore, the disposition effect can partially be explained by the concepts of selective decision making as well as regret avoidance. The mental attachment to arguments for having bought a stock – also known as the commitment towards an investment – delays the process of selling loss-generating stocks. The stronger the commitment towards an investment, the longer it takes to reason that the previously made decision to buy was wrong. In cases of doubt, the investor could even hold the loss-generating stocks, due to the fact that the active confession of misjudgment causes a stronger discomfiture than passiveness (Bergold and Mayer 2005, Tvede 2002).

---

[9] Odean (1998) examined 10'000 randomly chosen portfolios during 1987 and 1993 and comes to the conclusion that the disposition effect exists . Weber and Camerer (1998) confirm Odeans conclusion with further experimental analysis.

4.2.2. Stock Market Anomalies

Stock market anomalies are the observable result of market inefficiencies, caused by individual anomalies concerning the investors' behavior within the investment process.

Figure 5 overviews the most important capital market anomalies with their respective definition:

Anomaly	Definition
Overreaction/ underreaction	Stocks prices tend to overreact/underreact to new fundamental information (Barberis et al. 1998, De Bond and Thaler 1985, Neale and Northcraft 1987, Samuelson and Zeckhauser 1988).
Excess volatility	Stock price movements are higher than could be justified by fundamental reasons (Campell and Shiller 1988, LeRoy and Porter 1981, Shiller 1981, West 1988).
Announcement effect	Stock price changes in reaction to announcements tend to be late and exceed the fundamentally justified extent (Haugen 1999).
Herding	Investors are susceptible to the behavior of a broad group, because they are frightened of standing and failing alone (Shiller 2001).
Momentum hypothesis	Stocks that have been increasing in the past will continue increasing during the next six to twelve months, and vice versa (Jegadeesh and Titman 1993, Schiereck 1999).
Mean reversion	Stock prices tend to move in cycles (Antoniou et al 2007, Dean 1998, Kiehling 2001, Peterson 2007, Shiller 2001).
Winner-loser effect	The losers of the past will be the winners of the future, and vice versa (De Bond and Thaler 1985, Shefrin 2002).
Price-book-ratio effect	Stocks with a low PBR ratio generate higher returns than stock with a high PBR (Ball 1978, Daniel et al. 2001, Fama and French 1992).

Table 5: Stock Market Anomalies

Stock market prices tend to overreact to new fundamental information, which partially explains the higher than fundamentally justified volatility on stock markets – the so called excess volatility (Campell and Shiller 1988, LeRoy and Porter 1981, Shiller 1981, West 1988).

Excess volatility can also be explained by the announcement effect that assumes investors to initially react late to new fundamental information. Subsequently to this underreaction, stock prices tend to overshoot to an extent that exceeds the fundamentally justified value (Barberis et al 1998).

The overshooting of stock prices can be partially traced back to herding effects. The social psychologist Solomon Asch reported an experiment in 1952 that proved the immense power of social pressure generated by a group based on individual judgments – the herding effect (Shiller 2000). It describes the phenomena that investors tend to follow a broad group, because they are frightened of standing and failing alone.

The herding effect goes along with the momentum effect. Jegadeesh and Titman (1993) empirically proved that stocks, which have been increasing in the previous three to twelve months, will continue increasing during the next three to twelve months in the future, and vice versa.

Considering a period that clearly exceeds twelve months – e.g. a period that extends over three to five years – the contrary effect can be observed. Examinations by De Bond and Thaler (1985) showed that previous losers outperform the previous winners in the long run – the so called winner-loser effect. The combination of the momentum effect and the winner-loser effect lead to the concept of mean reversion (Antoniou et al. 2007), assuming that stock prices fluctuate in cycles (Dean 1998, Kiehling 2001, Peterson 2007, Shiller 2001).

Another stock market anomaly is the price-book-ratio effect, which states that stocks with a low PBR will outperform those with a high PBR (Ball 1978, Daniel et al. 2001, Fama and French 1992).

4.3. Sentiment Indicators

Sentiment indicators pursue the objective of transferring qualitative cognitions of the separate behavioral finance theories into measurable and aggregated stock market figures (Rose 2006, Hübner and Hussy 2006). Therefore, sentiment indicators measure how strongly actual stock market prices are influenced by behavioral factors – such as the market participants' prevailing mood or attitude towards actual events (Rüppel 2005).

Considering that the extent of behavioral influencing factors on stock market prices change over time, the measurement by which and to which extent stock market participants are driven by those behavioral factors, should enable the investor to draw a conclusion on whether or not phases of exaggeration are prevailing (Hübner 2003, Rose 2006).

In addition thereto, sentiment indicators not only measure the prevailing impact of behavioral influencing factors, but also the drivers of the prevailing market participants' behavior (Hübner 2003, Rose 2006). Therefore, an examination about to which extent investors are engaged in the stock market or which investors – private or professionals – are responsible for the prevailing stock market constellation (Hübner 2003).

Consequently, sentiment indicators can serve as a timing tool in terms of identifying phases of exaggeration, leading to the conclusion that sentiment indicators are categorized between the concepts of behavioral finance and technical analysis (Rose 2006).

With regard to the data generating process, sentiment indicators are distinguished between market data-based indicators and survey-based indicators (Rose 2006). Market data-based sentiment indicators can be derived by examining given market data – e.g. the ratio of the total invested amount of puts and calls, the so called put-call-ratio (Morlock 1995, Rübsamen 2004) –, whereas survey-based indicators are generated by interviewing potential market participants, e.g. the Ifo survey (Rose 2006).

4.4. Empirical Studies

The following empirical studies about the evidence of behavioral finance are evaluated by two steps. In a first step, the basis concept of behavioral finance[10] – Kahnemans and Tversky's prospect theory – is evaluated. In a second step, the most important stock market anomalies are taken into consideration by evaluating their occurrence as well as the possibility of creating strategies to exploit their occurrence.

Kahnemans and Tversky's prospect theory can be examined by considering empirical studies about the evidence of the theory's derived concepts – the reference point effect, loss aversion and the disposition effect.

The reference point effect as well as the connected effect of loss aversion are examined and empirically proven by Staw (1976), Shefrin and Statman (1985), Ferris et al. (1988), Camerer and Weber (1991) as well as Odean (1998). The disposition effect – as the aggregated result of the reference point and the loss aversion effect – is empirically proven by Heilmann et al. (2000).

---

[10] Historically considered.

With regard to the respective results of the most important stock market anomalies – overreaction/underreaction[11], announcement effect[12], excess volatility[13], herding[14], and winner-loser effect[15] - a conclusion can be drawn that their existence can be considered as empirically proven. At least the stock market anomalies of overreaction/underreaction, excess volatility, herding and the winner-loser effect are appropriate for creating a strategy enabling the investor to exploit its occurrence.

The empirical evidence of the price-book-ratio effect (see Section 3.3.) as well as the momentum-hypothesis (see Section 5.3.) is examined within the other respective chapters.

Summing up the results of the empirical studies about the prospect theory as well as the respective stock market anomalies, we can draw the conclusion that the concept of behavioral finance can be considered as empirically proven.

---

[11] Examinations by De Bondt and Thaler (1985, 1987), Berry and Dreman (1995), Fama and French (1992), Lakonishok et al. (1994) as well as Loughran and Ritter (1996) have shown that stocks tend to overreact.
Michaely et al. (1995) states that reactions to dividend cuts continue for an irrationally long period of time. Ikenberry et al. (1995) prove that investors underreact to stock repurchase programs.
[12] Abarbanell and Bernard (1992) prove that analysts underreact to earnings announcements. Chan et al. (1996) show that stock prices react gradually to earnings news.
[13] Cuthbertson and Hyde (2002) examine the excess volatility for the German and French stock market during 1973 and 1996 by applying the Campell-Shiller VAR (1988). They come to the conclusion that excess volatility exists in both markets.
[14] Lakonishok et al. (1992) and Wermers (1999) find weak evidence of pension fund managers herding. Grinblatt et al. (1995) find that the majority of mutual funds tend to invest with the crowd. Graham (1999) proves that investment newsletters herd. Welch (2000) proves that analysts are subjected to weak but significant herding behavior.
[15] DeBondt and Thaler (1985) examined the returns of winner and loser portfolios in the American stock market during 1926-1982. Considering a period of three to five years, the trend reversal of previous winner or loser portfolios is significant. Stock (1990), Schiereck and Weber (1995) as well as Bromann et al. (1997) examine the German stock market and come to the conclusion that the winner-loser effect exists . In addition to that, they state that the winner-loser effect can be exploited via respective investment strategies.

4.5. SWOT Analysis

In the following, the respective strengths, weaknesses, opportunities and threats to the concept of behavioral finance are explained:

- Strengths:
  - Empirical studies have proven that stock market participants do not behave rationally, but rather irrationally. Behavioral finance theories are based on the assumption of market participants behaving irrationally. Thus, behavioral phenomena – e.g. overconfidence, control of illusion, adaptation of mass opinions, and reversal of risk willingness – resulting in capital market anomalies, can be explained.
  - Stock market participants that deal with behavioral finance can coach themselves to behave more rationally (Fleing 2003) or even exploit the irrationality of other market participants – especially during boom and crash phases – due to the awareness of the factors that drive market participants to behave irrationally.
  - Behaviorally-driven timing indicators – so called sentiment indicators – enable stock market investors to draw a conclusion on how far actual stock prices are driven by psychological influencing factors. They can serve as tools for predicting the probability of future crashes or booms in the stock market.

- Weaknesses:
  - The most significant weakness of the behavioral finance approach is its fragmentation. There are a number of separate behavioral theories that explain the individual behavior of stock market participants, but actually, no aggregated synthesis concept of all of those separate individual theories has been developed yet (Hotz 2005).
  - The aggregation of individual irrationalities to a representative and meaningful figure is difficult. Sentiment indicators try to analyze the stock market participants' irrationalities on an aggregated basis, but their expressiveness in order to explain separate behavioral finance theories actually remains restricted (Poget and Wuerth 2007).
  - The observable stock market anomalies are difficult to measure in concrete figures (Wuerth and Poget 2007). That would be the basis for a systematic

prediction tool, enabling investors to time their stock investments by considering the occurrence probability of future stock market anomalies (Hotz 2005).
- Behavioral finance is not able to calculate a fair stock price.

- Opportunities:
  - The development of a synthesis concept which unifies the separate behavioral finance theories would be an important step towards explaining stock market anomalies on an aggregated scientific level.
  - The development of tools, enabling investors to measure market participants' irrationalities in concrete values – the basis for timing indicators – would be another important progression for behavioral finance. (Wuerth and Poget 2007). Approaches like sentiment indicators already follow this objective, but still have to be advanced. Therefore behavioral finance could be supplemented by technical analysis in order to improve its timing capabilities.
  - Behavioral finance pursues the objective of drawing conclusions by which and to which extent stock market prices are influenced by behavioral factors. However, it does not calculate a fair stock price. Therefore, it is dependent on the calculation of an intrinsic value – calculated by fundamentally-driven analysis concepts.

- Threats:
  - Assuming that the rationality of stock market participants or the EMH can undoubtedly be proven, behavioral finance would no longer generate any advantages (Hotz 2005).
  - Assuming that irrationality is not rationally predictable – arguing that otherwise, it would be rational – behavioral finance would not be able to develop tools that are able to predict future irrationalities (Hotz 2005).
  - Assuming that future examinations come to the result that separate behavioral finance theories could not be aggregated to a closed synthesis concept, the quantitative-based application of behavioral finance cognitions – in order to predict future stock market anomalies – would be weakened.

4.5. Preliminary Conclusion

Empirical studies have proven that stock markets are subjected by recurring anomalies. Important stock market anomalies – e.g. overreaction/underreaction, announcement effect, excess volatility, herding, and winner-loser effect – are temporarily occurring divergences between actual stock market prices and its intrinsic values, caused by stock market participants' irrational behavior during the investment process.

Those irrationalities cannot be explained by concepts assuming stock market participants to act rationally, so that behavioral finance is necessary to supplement rationally-based analysis concepts by psychological and sociological realizations, in order to explain as well as predict stock market anomalies.

Depending on which point in time irrationalities occur during the investment process, the separate behavioral finance theories can be differentiated by anomalies during information perception, information treatment and decision making. Those anomalies lead to stock market inefficiencies, observable by the occurrence of stock market anomalies.

Empirical studies have proven that stock market anomalies are recurring and exploitable, so that the necessity of a behavioral analysis approach like behavioral finance is scientifically and practically justified.

Nevertheless, the aggregation of qualitative cognitions of the separate behavioral finance theories to a closed overall behavioral finance concept has not yet been achieved. The quantitative measurement of stock market anomalies is limited on sentiment indicators that try to measure what and to which extent actual stock market prices are driven by irrational influencing factors.

Consequently, behavioral finance supplements rationally-driven analysis concepts with qualitative explanations, as to why divergences between real stock price developments and fundamentally justified values can occur, as well as making stock market anomalies quantitatively measurable by applying sentiment indicators. Taking these aspects into consideration, behavioral finance is an important analysis concept for explaining irrationalities on the stock market that cannot be explained by the prevailing analysis methods, but has to be advanced in terms of its closeness to an overall behavioral concept as well as its practical applicability by delivering quantitatively measurable values.

5. Technical Analysis

5.1. Definition and Premises

Technical analysis has its origin at the end of the 19th century, when Charles Dow and Edward Jones developed the idea of measuring the economic health of a country, by building up an index that is calculated by the average price of the most important companies' stock prices (Bassetti et al. 2007, Dahlquist and Kirkpatrick 2007, Murphy 1999).

With regard to company evaluation, Dow's and Jones's idea means that the value of a company can be analyzed by just considering its stock price (Rübsamen 2004). As such, technical analysis assumes that the stock market price – as the result of investors' demand and supply – is the only meaningful figure for evaluating a company (Pring 2002).

According to Murphy (1999, p.1), "Technical Analysis is the study of market action, preliminary trough the use of charts, for the purpose of forecasting future price trends." The term "market action" includes three principal sources of information – price, volume and open interest (Murphy 1999) – enabling the technical analyst to "identify a trend reversal at a relatively early stage and ride on that trend until the weight of the evidence shows or proves that the trend has reversed" (Pring 2002, p.3).

In order to be able to draw such a conclusion on the future company's stock price development, technical analysis is based on three basic premises that are considered as being fulfilled by the advocates of technical analysis (Murphy 1999):

- Stock market action discounts everything:
  Technical analysis assumes that fundamental as well as behavioral influencing factors – explicitly analyzed by fundamental analysis or behavioral finance – are already reflected by actual stock market prices, so that the explicit consideration and analysis of those factors does not enable the investor to generate any advantages (Pring 2002).
  Technical analysis assumes that the influence and interdependencies of fundamental and behavioral influencing factors on stock market prices are such complicated, that investors are not able to evaluate those factors correctly by analyzing their impacts on stock market prices (Williams 1998). Unlike fundamental analysis and behavioral finance, technical analysis only

considers stock market prices (as the overall evaluation of all important information influencing the company's value) to be appropriate for evaluating a company's value (Rübsamen 2004). Therefore, technical analysis does not deny fundamental and behavioral factors, nor does it assume that the explicit evaluation of those factors – e.g. the calculation of an intrinsic value – lead to advantages in order to outperform the market (Williams 1998).

- Stock prices move in trends:

Technical analysis assumes stock market prices – except from randomly price movements in the short run – to move in trends in the mid and long run (Rübsamen 2004). In contrast to randomly price movements in the short run, a trend expresses the direction of the market in the mid and long run (Murphy 1999).

With the assumption that "a trend in motion is more likely to continue than to reverse" (Murphy 1999, p.4), the analysis of actual stock price movements enables technical analysts to draw a conclusion on future stock price movements (Bassetti et al. 2007, Dahlquist and Kirkpatirck 2007). The assumption of the likelihood of trend continuation is based on natural scientific cognitions – e.g. Newton's first law of motion, which states that an object's inertia induces a higher likelihood that the objective will continue to follow the prevailing direction than to reverse (Murphy 1999).

Unlike fundamental analysis, technical analysis does not try to evaluate whether or not a company is undervalued or overvalued by comparing its intrinsic value and its actual market price, but rather it tries to evaluate whether a stock price trend will continue or reverse (Covel 2004, Dahlquist and Kirkpatrick 2007). Therefore, the identification and evaluation of the trend continuations, as well as reversals, enables technical analysts to generate an abnormal return by using technical analysis methods to time their investments (Dahlquist and Kirkpatrick 2007).

- History repeats itself:

Technical analysis assumes that the investors' reaction to certain events in the past – causing changes in demand and supply of stocks, expressed by certain chart patterns (Pring 1993) – are extensively stable over time, due to psychologically stable influencing factors on the investor's investment decisions (Plummer 2006). Therefore, it is assumed that historical chart patterns – expressing a certain event in the past – are appropriate for being used to predict future price movements, due to the assumption that investors will behave similarly in the future if comparable events should occur (Pring 2002).

5.2. Analysis Methods

Technical analysis is not just composed of company evaluation "through the use of charts" (Murphy 1999, p. 4), but also by applying more mathematically-driven concepts – the technical indicators (Cesar 1996).

Consequently, technical analysis is subdivided into two interdependent approaches, known as chart analysis and technical indicators (Cesar 1996). Chart analysis focuses on the examination of visualized data (Murphy 1996), whereas technical indicators concentrate on statistically-driven analysis methods of stock data (Vieker 1996).

With regard to the scientific demand of this thesis, the following examinations are focused on technical indicators, which are – unlike in a chart analysis – appropriate for examinations in terms of their empirical verifiability (Aronson 2007).

5.2.1. Chart Analysis

A chart analysis can be considered as the historical foundation of technical analysis (Kaufmann 1998) and compounds all technical analysis methods that try to predict future stock price movements by evaluating historical stock price data visualized by charts (Murphy 1996).

With regard to Dahlquist and Kirkpatrick's (2007, p.191) definition, "charts are merely graphical displays of data."

In order to be able to evaluate those charts, two successive work steps have to be executed by the chartist. First, market data – price, volume and if available open interest – has to be visualized by charts (Murphy 1999). Secondly, the generated charts are analyzed in terms of characteristics that could deliver an indication on future stock price development (Murphy 1999).

The majority of chart techniques – besides point and figure charting neglecting the time period (Zieg 1997) – present the considered time period and traded volume on the horizontal axis, whereas stock prices are shown on the vertical axis (Murphy 1999). Depending on how market data is visualized, chart techniques are distinguished between line charts, bar charts[16], candlesticks charts, and point and figure charts (Florek 2000).

In addition to that, charts can be differentiated by weekly, monthly and even yearly charts, depending on the visualized time period (Murphy 1996).

Figure 7 shows a monthly bar chart of the BMW AG from 01-01-2006 to 12-31-2007, on which the respective chart analysis tools for evaluating the future stock price movements are already applied:

Figure 7: Chart Analysis Applied to the BMW AG

No matter which chart tool is considered, all of them follow the same overall objective: determining if a prevailing trend will be continue or reverse, in order to be able to exploit the knowledge of the future trend direction for respective positioning (Dahlquist and Kirkpatrick 2007).

Still, how is a trend defined? According to Murphy (1999, p.49), "In a general sense, the trend is simply the direction of the market, which way it's moving." In a

---

[16] In the following, the respective charts are visualized by the bar chart technique, due to its predominant use in practice (Murphy 1999). With reference to Murphy's definition (1999, p.36), "It's called a bar chart because each day's range is represented by a vertical bar. The bar chart shows the open, high, low and closing prices. The tic to the right of the vertical bar is the closing price. The opening price is the tic to the left bar."

closer sense, stock market movements are characterized by a series of zigzags. "These zigzags are the result of successive series of peaks and troughs. It is the direction of those peaks and troughs that constitutes market trends." (Murphy 1999, p.49).

Depending on whether those peaks and troughs are moving up, down, or sideways, trends are distinguished between uptrend, downtrend or sideways trend (Bassetti et al. 2007, Pring 2002). According to Murphy (1999, p.50), "An uptrend would be defined as a series of successively higher peaks and troughs; a downtrend is just the opposite, a series of declining peaks and troughs: horizontal peaks and troughs would identify a sideways price trend."

In the following, the respective analysis tools for identifying which trend is actually prevailing, or for predicting if the prevailing trend will be continuing or reversing, are distinguished between basic concepts (Section 5.2.1.1.) and formation analysis (Section 5.2.1.2.).

5.2.1.1. Basic Concepts

Market trends are the result of successive peaks and troughs, but what determines the price level at which peaks and troughs are established?

In order to be able to explain those phenomena, the terms of support and resistance are introduced. The troughs are called support, whereas the peaks are called resistance (Bassetti et al. 2007).

The term support describes a price level or area on the chart where demand exceeds supply so that decline is stopped and prices turn back up again (Bassetti et al. 2007, Murphy 1999, Pring 2002). In analogy to that, resistance is a price level or area on the chart, where supply exceeds demand, so that increase is stopped and prices go down again (Bassetti et al. 2007, Murphy 1999, Pring 2002). Looking at Figure 7, we can conclude that a support level of approximately 40€, as well as a resistance level of approximately 45 € (blue lines), were established. Chart analysis tries to use those support and resistance levels by assuming that the extrapolation of previous support and resistance levels enables the chartist to come to a conclusion, at which price level future stock prices will stop decreasing or increasing (Bassetti et al. 2007).

Looking at the support and resistance level in Figure 7, we can come to two other further important assumptions of chart analysis. Firstly, previous resistance levels (February 2006) that have once been significantly breached become support levels

(December 2006, March, November, December 2007) and vice versa (Bassetti et al. 2007, Murphy 1999). Secondly, breaches of previous resistance or support levels are more significant the more they go along with a high trading volume (March 2006, September 2007) (Bassetti et al. 2007, Dahlquist and Kirkpatrick 2007).

In addition to support and resistance levels, chartists examine a chart in terms of the existence of trend lines and trend channels. Depending on the trend direction, trend lines are distinguished between up trend and down trend lines (Bassetti et al. 2007, Murphy 1999, Pring 2002). According to Murphy (1999, p.64), "An up trend line is a straight line drawn upward to the right along successive reaction lows" (lower red up trend line) whereas "A down trend line is drawn downward to the right along successive rally peaks." (Higher green downtrend line). Chart analysis tries to use up trend or downtrend lines by extrapolating their development in the future, in order to be able to time optimal investment points within the prevailing trend – represented by prices that are tangent to the trend line (June to September 2006; February to March 2007) – or to determine trend reversals if a trend line is significantly breached (March 2007) (Dahlquist and Kirkpatrick 2007).

Trend channels are established if an uptrend or downtrend moves within a certain range of two trend lines (June to September 2006; February to March 2007), which enables the chartist to trade within the given range of the trend channel (Bassetti et al. 2007, Murphy 1999).

5.2.1.2. Formation Analysis

Within chart analysis, the terms "formation" and "pattern" are used interchangeably (Dahlquist and Kirckpatrick 2007). According to Dahlquist and Kirckpatrick's (2007, p. 302) definition, "A pattern is simply a configuration of price action that is bounded, above and below, by some form of either a line or a curve. The lines that bind price movement in a pattern can be trend lines or support/resistance lines." Those patterns have predictive value in terms of determining whether a prevailing trend will be continuing or reverse (Bassetti et al. 2007, Pring 2002).

Depending on whether a pattern predicts the continuation or reversal of a prevailing trend, patterns are distinguished between continuation and reversal patterns (Murphy 1999).

Reversal patterns are usually differentiated by five categories (Murphy 1999): the head and shoulders, triple tops and bottoms, double tops and bottoms, spike (or V) tops and bottoms, and the saucer (or rounding) pattern (Bulkowski 2006).

Figures 7 shows that the prevailing up trend reversed after the appearance of a triple top (yellow circle, March to April 2006), or a head and shoulder formation (yellow circle, May to July 2007). A triple top is established by three peaks at the same price level (Bulkowski 2006), whereas the head and shoulder formation "gets its name from its resemblance to a head with two shoulders on either side" (Achelis 1995, p.224, Bulkowski 2006). Sometimes the differentiation between triple tops and head and shoulder formations is quite difficult in practice, but does not matter in terms of its expressiveness, due to the fact that both formations indicate a trend reversal (Bassetti et al. 2007, Murphy 1999).

Continuation patterns are usually differentiated between triangles, flags, pennants, and wedges (Murphy 1999). Figure 7 shows that the prevailing down trend was continued after the appearance of a descending triangle (pink triangle, September to October 2007).

The descending triangle is characterized by stock prices that move within a range, determined by an uptrend line and a lower flat line (Achelis 1995). The downside signal is triggered by a significant closure under the lower flat line, usually on increased trading volume (November 2007) (Murphy 1999).

5.2.2. Indicator Analysis

Indicator analysis can be considered as the modern subset of technical analysis. It compounds all of the methods that evaluate historical stock data by applying statistical analysis concepts (Cesar 1996).

Technical indicators enable the technician to evaluate whether a trend is prevailing as well as whether a phase of exaggeration is indicated (Cesar 1996, Florek 2000).

Assuming that the stock market is subjected to an uptrend or downtrend, trend following indicators are used in order to follow the trend as long as its strength is indicated as being strong (Lindner and Müller 2007). This is due to the assumption that a trend is more likely to continue than to reverse, until there is evidence for a trend reversal. Evidence of a trend reversal is received if a trend-following indicator shows a weakening in trend strength (Covel 2004, Florek 2000). Should there be a weakening trend oscillators are also considered, in order to be able to draw a conclusion as to whether or not the trend weakening takes place during a phase of exaggeration (Rübsamen 2004, Schwager 1998). Oscillators give an impression of how strongly the stock market is overbought or oversold (Lindner and Müller 2007, Schwager 1998).

If a trend weakening takes place during a phase of exaggeration, the likelihood of a trend reversal is considered to be high, due to the fact that their will be no future demand (boom) or supply (crash) for a trend continuation (Murphy 1999). Figure 8 shows the application of trends following indicators as well as oscillators on the stock price development of the BMW AG from 01-01-2006 to 12-31-2007:

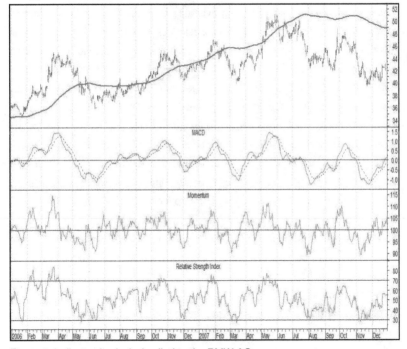

Figure 8: Indicator Analysis Applied to the BMW AG

Trend-following indicators are calculated on an absolute basis, whereas oscillators refer to a relative basis (Florek 2000). Therefore, trend-following indicators can theoretically achieve each value, whereas oscillators fluctuate within a given range of values (Lindner and Müller 2007).

In the following, technical indicators are explained by differentiating between trend-following indicators (Section 5.2.2.1.) and oscillators (Section 5.2.2.2.).

5.2.2.1. Trend-Following Indicators

Trend-following indicators pursue the objective of smoothening randomly short-term price movements in order to make a prevailing trend and its respective strength visible (Florek 2000, Lindner and Müller 2007). Consequently, trend-following indicators diminish price movements that are not subjected to a clear trend, but go along with the disadvantage of discovering a trend or trend reversal late.

The most commonly used trend-following indicator is the moving average (Florek 2000). A lot of trend following indicators – e.g. the MACD – are based on the basis concept of moving averages. Moving averages are calculated by the arithmetical average of a certain time period of historical stock prices (Kaufmann 1998, Rose 2006). The respective newest stock price substitutes the oldest stock price within the considered time period – therefore the average is considered to be moving.

The most commonly used moving averages are calculated by the arithmetical average of the last 38, 90 or 200 trading days (Murphy 1999, Rose 2006).

Figure 8 shows the 200 days moving average (red line within the chart) for the BMW stock. As long as the actual stock price does not cross the moving average significantly, the prevailing trend is considered to be intact (February until April 2006). As soon as the actual stock price crosses the moving average significantly, a trend reversal is to be assumed (May and September 2006) (Florek 2000).

If the actual stock price crosses the moving average from bottom to top, a buy signal is generated (September 2006), whereas a sell signal is generated, if the actual stock price crosses the moving average from top to bottom (May 2006) (Florek 2000).

Figure 8 shows another widely used following indicator – the MACD (Moving Average Convergence Divergence). The MACD was developed by Gerald Appel in 1979 and is calculated by subtracting two different exponentially moving averages and comparing the result with a signal line (Lohrbach and Schumann 1995). Therefore the exponentially moving average of 26 days is subtracted from the exponentially moving average of twelve days (Rose 2006). The result is the so called trend line (red line) which is compared with a signal line (black dashed line). The signal line is calculated by the exponentially moving average of nine days. The chosen time periods are derived by the length of short term stock market cycles observed by Appel (Rose 2006).

The MACD delivers trading signals by comparing the trend line with the signal line. If the trend line crosses the signal line from bottom to top, a buy signal is generated (e.g. March 2007), whereas a sell signal is generated, if the trend line crosses the signal line from top to bottom (e.g. April 2006) (Florek 2000, Rose 2006, Schwager 1998).

5.2.2. Oscillators

Oscillators pursue the objective of analyzing whether the stock market is actually overbought or oversold (Lindner and Müller 2007, Schwager 1998). Consequently, oscillators are relative indicators that put actual stock prices into relation to previous stock prices (Florek 2000). Due to its relative basis, the respective oscillator values fluctuate around their extreme values (Lindner and Müller 2007).

Unlike trend-following indicators, oscillators show a forerun characteristic in comparison to real stock price developments (Florek 2000).

The two most important oscillators are the momentum and the RSI (Relative Strength Index). The momentum measures the strength of stock price movements by visualizing the gradient of price movements within a certain period (Lindner and Müller 2007, Schwager 1998). Consequently the momentum of a stock is the difference of today's price compared to the price x-time periods ago (Florek 2000). Usually, a time period of ten or 25 days is made use of (Rose 2006).

Figure 8 shows the momentum for a time period of ten days (red line) that fluctuates around the neutral value of 100 (blue line). An increasing momentum beneath the neutral value of 100, is derived by a diminishing difference between the actual stock price and the price ten trading days ago, which indicates the weakening of a down trend (e.g. June 2006). An increasing momentum above the neutral value of 100 (blue line), is derived from the actual stock price that quotes the stock price ten trading days ago. The steeper the momentum's gradient, the more dynamic the actual trend is. However, the higher the momentum value, the more overbought a market is and thus, a trend reversal is also more likely (e.g. March 2007). Unlike momentum, the RSI – developed by Welles Wilder in 1978 – does not show the relative strength, but the inner strength of stock price developments (Florek 2000). Consequently the RSI is calculated by dividing the sum of increasing and decreasing stock prices within a certain time period – normally nine or fourteen days (Rose 2006). The result is the relative strength of the considered stock (Florek 2000). To generate the relative strength index, this result is put into a formula, in which 100 is subtracted by the quotient of 100 divided by 1 plus the calculated relative strength of the stock (Kaufmann 1998, Rose 2006).

Figure 8 shows the BMW stocks' relative strength for fourteen days (red line), oscillating around its theoretically achievable extreme values of 0 and 100 (Brown 1999). In practice, RSI values over 70 indicate that a stock is overbought (e.g. in March 2006) whereas RSI values under 30 indicate that a stock is oversold (e.g. in January 2007) (Sepiashvili 2004, Vieker 1996).

5.3. Empirical Studies

With regard to the empirical evidence of technical analysis, particularly empirical studies over the last thirty years have proven that the stock market does not move randomly (see Section 2.2). Therefore, technical analysis is theoretically able to generate an abnormal return in comparison to a simple buy-and-hold strategy, by predicting future stock market prices on the basis of historical stock market prices (Chan et al. 2000, Conrad and Kaul 1988, Lo and MacKinlay 1988).

Which concepts of technical analysis are empirically proven to be able to generate an abnormal return? The concept of chart analysis is strongly subjected to subjective interpretation possibilities and therefore, is not appropriate for scientific examinations (Aronson 2007). Consequently, the following overview of empirical studies about the evidence of technical analysis is focused on the concept of technical indicators – evaluated by considering the empirical results of the evidence of moving averages and momentum strategies.

The empirical results of studies about moving averages are ambiguous. Empirical studies for the American stock market show the superiority of simple moving averages[17], whereas examinations of the German stock market lead to the conclusion that MACD strategies are not capable of generating an abnormal return.[18] Consequently, at least the superiority of MACD strategies towards a simple buy-and-hold strategy is doubtful.

---

[17] Colby and Meyers (2002) examined a period from 1968 to 1986 and came to the conclusion that a moving average strategy is able to generate abnormal returns.
Brock et al. (1992) examined a period of 1897 to 1986, and proved that returns are higher on days when stock market prices lay above their moving averages, than on days when stock market prices lay below their moving averages.
[18] Brock (1994) as well as Gothein (1995) examined different MACD strategies from 1960 to 1990 or 1980 to 1990, and come to the conclusion, that the different MACD strategies are defeated by a simple buy-and-hold strategy.

With regard to the superiority of momentum strategies, we can determine that the broad majority of empirical studies have successfully proven their empirical evidence (Holtfort et al. 2007). German[19] and European stock markets[20], as well as the American stock market[21], show evidence of the superiority of momentum strategies, whereas the results for emerging markets are ambiguous.

By considering all aspects of empirical studies about the evidence of technical analysis, we can see that the superiority of chart analysis is not empirically verifiable, due to its strong impact of subjective interpretation possibilities, whereas the evidence of technical indicators can be considered to be empirically proven by at least some concepts – e.g. by the superiority of momentum strategies in comparison to a simple buy-and-hold strategy.

---

[19] Schiereck and Weber (1995, 2000) proved the superiority of momentum strategies for the German stock market during the examination period from 1973 to 1997.
Holfort et al. (2007) examined the superiority of a rolling momentum strategy in comparison with the average performance of the C-DAX during 1999-2006 and came to the conclusion that the rolling momentum strategy is able to generate an annual abnormal return of 14%.
In contrast to these results, Brock (1995) examined the German stock market from 1960 to 1990 and came to the conclusion that the average return of 27.45% of a RSI strategy clearly lies below the buy-and-hold strategy's average return of 50.40%.
[20] Rouwenhorst (1997) confirms the success of momentum strategies for twelve European stock markets.
[21] Rouwenhorst (1999) considers the momentum strategy to be proven on emerging markets, whereas Bekaert et al. (1997) states that at least momentum strategies do not succeed in all emerging markets.

5.4. SWOT Analysis

In the following, the respective strengths, weaknesses, opportunities and threats of the concept of technical analysis are explained:

- Strengths:
    - Unlike fundamental analysis and behavioral finance, technical analysis enables the investor to time his/her investment decision (Covel 2004, Murphy 1999).
    - Particularly technical indicators enable investors to get an impression as to what extent actual stock price movements lay within the average stock price range of previous periods. Consequently, potential phases of boom or crash can be identified by setting actual stock price movements in relation to historical averages.
    - Additional market data – e.g. traded volume and open interest – enables the investor to gain an impression on how investors are positioned.

- Weaknesses:
    - Technical analysis – particularly its subset chart analysis – is strongly influenced by subjective interpretation possibilities due to the fact that it is more driven by heuristic decision rules, based on practical experiences, than on scientifically proven theories. Therefore, it shows a lack in scientifically proven foundations that could be aggregated to a closed scientific theory (Hruby 1999).
    - Technical analysis is not able to evaluate whether or not a stock is undervalued or overvalued, due to one of its main assumptions that stock market action discounts everything. Technical analysis just considers how much actual stock prices differ from historical stock prices. Assuming that historical stock prices do not reflect the fundamental value of a company – at least to a certain extent – technical analysis does allow any conclusion on company value. Consequently, the expressiveness of technically-driven predictions about company value, are dependent upon market participants that do not just evaluate stocks in terms of technically-driven triggers, but by considering the theoretically justified fundamental value of a company – the fundamentals (Menz 2004).

- Opportunities:
  - The chaos theory shows some similarities with technical analysis (Covel 2004, Williams 1998). Due to the fact that the chaos theory is more solid in terms of its scientifically proven assumptions, technical analysis could try to support its practically-driven concepts via scientifically-driven cognitions of the chaos theory.
  - Some of the cognitions of behavioral finance – e.g. the reference point effect, herding effects, momentum effects and the winner-loser effect – could turn out to be appropriate for supporting concepts of technical analysis – e.g. long lasting trend patterns or successfully applied momentum strategies (Covel 2004, Dahlquist and Kirkpatrick 2007, Pring 1993).
  - The concept of technical analysis could be strengthened by acknowledging the necessity of fundamentally-driven analysis concepts in order to be able to generate stock market prices that approximately reflect fundamentally justified values.

- Threats:
  - If at least the weak form of market efficiency could be proven without a doubt, the investor would not be able to generate steady excess returns by applying technical analysis (Aronson 2007, Menz 2004, Niquet 1997).
  - In order to be able to predict future stock market developments by considering historical stock market prices, the considered time periods have to meet some statistical criteria – e.g. statistical stationarity – to be comparable. In reality, stock market prices often do not fulfill the criteria of stationarity, so that the statistical attributes change over time, which puts the expressiveness of technical forecasts into question (Menz 2004).

5.5. Preliminary Conclusion

Empirical studies over the last thirty years have shown that the stock market does not move randomly, such that historical stock price movements can be used for making determinations on future stock price developments.

The predictability of future stock price movements, by analyzing historical stock prices, is the main assumption of technical analysis. It is based on three premises: stock market action discounts everything, stock prices move in trends and history repeats itself. Assuming that these three premises are fulfilled, the application of technical analysis enables stock market investors to generate an abnormal return by just considering historical stock prices.

Depending on whether historical stock prices are analyzed visually or statistically, technical analysis is differentiated by chart analysis and technical indicators. Empirical studies have proven that at least some technical indicator concepts – e.g. the momentum strategy – enable stock market investors to generate an abnormal return in comparison to a simple buy-and-hold strategy. In contrast to that, chart analysis is strongly influenced by subjective interpretation possibilities, preventing it from being examined empirically.

Considering the concept of technical analysis as a whole, we can conclude that technical analysis has its strengths in enabling investors to time their stock investments. Fundamental analysis as well as behavioral finance just evaluates a time period during which a stock is undervalued or overvalued respectively, giving advice to what extent stock market participants are subjected by non-rational influencing factors, but technical analysis is able to determine the exact point in time when a stock should be bought or sold.

Nevertheless, chart analysis is lacking in scientifically-proven foundations – particularly the subset of chart analysis – causing for technically-derived investment decisions to be characterized by subjective interpretation possibilities.

With regard to the opportunities of technical analysis, scientifically proven cognitions of the chaos theory as well as behavioral finance could be used to develop a more scientifically foundation of the techniques of technical analysis leading to a higher scientific acceptance.

6. Synthesis Capabilities of Fundamental Analysis, Behavioral Finance and Technical Analysis

6.1. Objective and Procedure

On the basis of the previously discovered realizations about fundamental analysis (Chapter 3.), behavioral finance (Chapter 4.) and technical analysis (Chapter 5.), the following chapter examines the synthesis capabilities of these three analysis concepts.

The objective of determining synthesis capabilities between fundamental analysis, behavioral finance and the technical analysis is, to eliminate the respective weaknesses of the separate analysis concept, by taking the respective strengths of the two other analysis concepts into consideration. In order to be able to derive appropriate synthesis capabilities between fundamental analysis, behavioral finance and technical analysis, the procedure is as follows:

In a first step, the theoretical synthesis capabilities are examined by combining the respective SWOT analyses of each analysis concept, in order to be able to draw a conclusion on the theoretical synthesis capabilities (Section 6.2.).

In a second step, the practical synthesis capabilities are empirically examined by the practical example of the DAX performance index (Section 6.3.).

Taking the theoretical as well as the practical synthesis capabilities of fundamental analysis, behavioral finance and technical analysis into consideration, a preliminary conclusion on the synthesis capabilities in general is made (Section 6.4.).

6.2. Theoretical Synthesis Capabilities

The combination of the previously made SWOT analyses of fundamental analysis (Section 3.4.), behavioral finance (Section 4.5.) and technical analysis (Section 5.4.) pursues the objective of eliminating the weaknesses of the respective analysis concept by taking the strengths of the two other analysis concepts into consideration.

In order to achieve this objective, the procedure for deriving the theoretical synthesis concept is as follows:

I. The possibilities of fundamental analysis, behavioral finance and technical analysis are taken into consideration, indicating the improvement capabilities of each analysis concept.

II. Based on step one, the respective strengths of fundamental analysis, behavioral finance and technical analysis are combined in a second step, ensuring that the theoretical synthesis concept is received.

III. Step three points out which weaknesses of the three analysis concepts have been successfully eliminated by combining their strengths.

IV. Finally, the threats of the developed theoretical analysis concept are derived by considering the threats of the three analysis concepts.

I. Considering the possibilities of fundamental analysis, behavioral finance and technical analysis:

- Fundamental Analysis:
  - Fundamental analysis could be supplemented by evaluation approaches that have their strengths in terms of providing a timing advice about, at which point in time, an undervalued or overvalued stock should be bought or sold.
  - Fundamental analysis could be supplemented by evaluation approaches that are not based on the assumption of rationally, but rather irrationally behaving market participants.
  - Fundamentally-driven stock market investors could be professionally coached in behavioral finance, aimed at the objective to become aware of the factors that drive investors to behave irrationally.

- Behavioral Finance:
  - Behavioral finance could be supplemented by technical analysis in order to improve its timing capabilities.
  - Behavioral finance pursues the objective of drawing conclusions about what and to which extent stock market prices are influenced by behavioral factors, but does not calculate a fair stock price. Therefore, it is dependent on the calculation of an intrinsic value – calculated by fundamentally-driven analysis concepts.

- Technical Analysis:
  - Some of the cognitions of behavioral finance – e.g. the reference point effect, herding effects, momentum effects and the winner-loser effect – are appropriate for supporting concepts of technical analysis – e.g. long lasting trend patterns or successfully applied momentum strategies.

- The concept of technical analysis could be strengthened by acknowledging the necessity of fundamentally-driven analysis concepts in order to be able to generate stock market prices that approximately reflect fundamentally justified values.

Taking the possibilities of the three analysis concepts into consideration, we can determine that fundamental analysis, behavioral finance and technical analysis do have supplemental capabilities that have to be analyzed in detail by evaluating their respective strengths.

II. Combining the respective strengths of fundamental analysis, behavioral finance and technical analysis to a synthesis concept:

- Fundamental Analysis:
  - The calculation of the intrinsic value of stock provides an indication on how far the actual stock market price reflects the fundamentally justified value.
  - Present value methods consider the respective value drivers of a company.
  - The company's value drivers are represented in models.
- Behavioral Finance:
  - Behavioral finance theories are based on the assumption of irrationally behaving market participants, so that the resulting models are able to explain capital market anomalies.
  - Stock market investors can be coached to behave more rationally – particularly during extreme market phases – in order to prevent cascade effects.
  - Behaviorally-driven timing indicators – so called sentiment indicators – enable stock market investors to draw a conclusion on how far actual stock prices are driven by psychologically influencing factors.
- Technical Analysis:
  - Technical analysis is able to determine the exact point in time in which a stock should be bought or sold.
  - Particularly technical indicators enable investors to get an impression to which extent actual stock price movements lay within the average stock price range of previous periods.

Taking the respective strengths of fundamental analysis, behavioral finance and technical analysis into consideration, we can determine the following about the content of the theoretical synthesis concept:

Calculating intrinsic values with present value methods – that evaluate the company's value drivers in models – enables investors not only to determine the fundamentally justified value of a stock, but also to gain an impression of how sensitive the intrinsic value of a stock reacts towards different influencing factors. By comparing the intrinsic value of the stock with the market prices of the stock, the investor is able to determine, which stock is fundamentally undervalued or overvalued and should therefore be bought or sold.

In the long-term, the stock market follows its intrinsic value, but in the short-term, the actual market price can diverge significantly from its intrinsic value – particularly during extreme market phases. The extreme market phases – e.g. booms or crashes – are characterized by irrationally acting stock market participants that do not primarily evaluate a stock by its intrinsic value, but by irrational motivations that cannot be explained by fundamental analysis (Aliber and Kindleberger 2005, Barton et al. 2003, El-Erian 2008).

In contrast to fundamental analysis, behavioral finance theories are based on the assumption of irrationally-behaving market participants, so that the resulting models are able to explain those capital market anomalies. Investors, who take behavioral finance additionally to fundamental analysis into considerarion, can profit by doing so for two reasons:

On the one hand, investors who have become aware of the reasons why market participants behave irrationally can coach themselves to behave rationally during extreme market phases.

On the other hand, the consideration of sentiment indicators enables investors to draw a conclusion, as to what extent and with what factors stock market participants behave irrationally. This is the basis for being able to draw a conclusion about at which point in time irrational market phases have achieved their climax. This makes it possible to know when stock market participants can be expected to refocus on fundamentally-driven influencing factors. This is an essential requirement for investing into fundamentally undervalued or overvalued stocks. Fundamental analysis only succeeds, if other stock market participants recognize the undervaluation or overvaluation of a stock during a given investment period. Consequently, fundamentally-driven investors have to notice if stock market participants will behave rationally, and therefore discover the undervaluation or overvaluation of a stock, during the scheduled investment period.

In addition to the strengths of fundamental analysis and behavioral finance, technical analysis can be used by the investor for two reasons:

Firstly, to get an impression as to what extent actual stock price movements lie within the average stock price range of previous periods. Secondly, technical analysis enables investors to time their investment decisions. Particularly technical indicators enable investors to get an impression to what extent actual stock price movements lay within the average stock price range of previous periods and thus, can point out phases of exaggeration. Consequently, technical indicators are appropriate for timing an investment decision by being able to determine the climax of phases of exaggeration.

III. Successfully eliminated weaknesses of the respective analysis concepts:

- Fundamental Analysis:
  - Inability to determine at which point in time the evaluated stock should be bought or sold.
  - Inability to determine at which point in time stock market participants discover the undervaluation or overvaluation of a stock.
  - Inability to explain stock market anomalies by assuming stock market participants to behave rationally.
- Behavioral Finance:
  - Behavioral finance has a lack of timing capabilities.
  - Behavioral finance is not able to calculate a fair stock price.
- Technical Analysis:
  - Technical analysis is not able to evaluate whether or not a stock is undervalued or overvalued.

Taking the successfully eliminated weaknesses of the three analysis concepts into consideration, the following can be determined: the synthesis concept is not appropriate for eliminating all of the weakness of the respective analysis approaches (compare with the SWOT analyses in the respective chapter), but is at least able to eliminate some of the main weaknesses of each analysis concept.

IV. Threats from the developed synthesis concept:

The combination of the respective strengths of fundamental analysis, behavioral finance and technical analysis results in a weakened susceptibility towards changing influencing factors on the stock market, ones that could destroy the predictive capabilities of the synthesis concept.

Nevertheless, the main threats to the predictive capabilities of the developed synthesis concept still remain. Assuming that the EMH or at least the semi-efficient stock market form can be scientifically proven to be permanently existent, the developed synthesis concept would not generate any advantages for investors in terms of predicting future stock price developments.

6.3. Practical synthesis capabilities using the example of the DAX Performance Index

In order to be able to determine whether and to which extent fundamental analysis, behavioral finance and technical analysis are appropriate in practically supplementing each other with their respective strengths, the respective strengths and weaknesses of each analysis concept must first be analyzed by a practical empirical study. Afterwards, the respective practical synthesis capabilities can be determined on the basis of the result of this study.

Consequently, the practical advantages or disadvantages of calculating the intrinsic value (Section 6.3.1.1.), sentiment indicators (Section 6.3.1.2.) and technical indicators (Section 6.3.1.3.) are examined as part of an empirical study that has been conducted by the author.

The empirical study refers to the DAX performance index (ISIN: DE0008469008)[22] and encompasses a time period of 58 months – 1-1-2004 to 10-31-2008. The DAX is determined by considering the stock price developments of the thirty largest and most traded German blue chip companies that are approved in the Prime Standard[23]. The DAX was chosen as the basis of the empirical study, because of

---

[22] In the following the DAX performance index will just be called DAX.
[23] The prime standard is the stock segment with the highest transparency standards within the stock segment systematic of the Deutsche Börse AG.

its strong diversification and qualitatively assured database, offered by the Deutsche Börse AG. Therefore, randomly driven influencing factors, that could restrict the discoveries of the empirical study, have been eliminated as much as possible by choosing the DAX.

With regard to the following examinations, the composition as well as the calculation of the DAX has to first be considered:

The composition of the DAX has been dynamically changing from 1-1-2004 to 10-31-2008, so that changes in composition have to be taken into consideration – e.g. for calculating the intrinsic value of the DAX (Section 6.3.3.1.)

Table 7 in the appendix alphabetically shows all 34 DAX members during the examined time period, whereby the orange marked fields indicate a change.

In addition to that, an understanding of how the DAX is calculated will be necessary in order to be able to understand the calculation of its intrinsic value (Section 6.3.3.1.). The DAX is calculated according to the Laspeyres formula set out below (Deutsche Börse AG 2008):

$$Index_t = K_T * \frac{\sum\limits_{i=1}^{n} p_{it} * q_{iT} * ff_{iT} * c_{it}}{\sum\limits_{i=1}^{n} p_{io} * q_{io}} * Base.$$

Whereby:

c_{it} = Correction factor of stock class i at time t

ff_{iT} = Free float factor of stock class i at time T

n = Number of stock in the index

p_{io} = Closing price of stock i on the trading day before the first inclusion in an index of Deutsche Börse

p_{it} = Price of stock i at time t

q_{io} = Number of stock of stock class i on the trading day before the first inclusion in an index of Deutsche Börse

q_{iT} = Number of stock of stock class i at time T

K_T = Index-specific changing factor valid as of changing date T

T = Date of last chaining.

6.3.1. Practical Application of Fundamental Analysis, Behavioral Finance and Technical Analysis

6.3.1.1. Intrinsic Value

With regard to practical examinations, to answer the question as to whether and especially to which extent stock price movements reflect a company's intrinsic value, a comparison must be made between the company's stock price movements and its theoretically justified intrinsic values over time.

However, it is difficult to determine the intrinsic value of a stock, due to the fact that it is difficult to determine which figure measures the intrinsic value objectively.

Consequently, the average target price of all fundamentally-driven equity analysts' recommendations within the considered period was calculated, such that subjectively distorted evaluation divergences are weakened. Therefore, the following empirical study encompasses 12'462 analyst recommendations for all stock listed in the DAX performance index from 1-1-2004 and 31-10-2008[24]. In order to be able to calculate an intrinsic value, it is assumed that the analysts' recommendations are based on fundamentally-driven analysis concepts. The distribution of the 12'462 analyst recommendations employed within the empirical study is alphabetically shown in Table 8 in the appendix.

The intrinsic value of the DAX is composed of the respective intrinsic values of the thirty stock included within the DAX. Depending on the weight of the respective stock, each stock has a differently strong impact on the overall intrinsic value of the DAX. Consequently, it's not only the stocks' intrinsic values that have to be considered, but also the respective weighing factors of each stock. In order to clarify the procedure of calculating the intrinsic value of the DAX, the calculation process is subdivided into two steps – calculating the stocks' average intrinsic value per month (I.) and weighing the respective stock's intrinsic value (II.):

---

[24] The analyst recommendations are based on Bloomberg database and were corrected by evident data base failure, if necessary. An overview of the employed 12'462 analyst recommendations is provided in excel sheet "DAX Performance Index - Intrinsic Value", Tab "1. Overview Recommendations". This is available on the attached CD.

I. Calculation of the stocks' average intrinsic value per month:

In a first step, the intrinsic value of every one of the thirty stock included within the DAX has to be determined for a specific time period. Taking into consideration that the calculation of an intrinsic value for each trading day and for every one of the thirty stocks would exceed the extent of this thesis, the intrinsic value calculation is limited to an average intrinsic value per month for each stock. Therefore, the arithmetic average of one month is calculated for all analyst recommendations for a stock within a month.[25]

However, the analysts' stock target prices have to be modified at their hight if stock splittings occur. With regard to the following weighing of the stocks intrinsic value (see Chapter 2.), all stock splittings concerning the stocks included in the DAX during the considered time period have to be taken into consideration. Consequently, the stock's target price gets divided according to the respective stock split ratio. With regard to the weighing factors of the Deutsche Börse AG, it is not decisive when the real stock splitting was executed, but when the stock splitting was taken into consideration by the Deutsche Börse AG for calculating the DAX. Table 6 in the appendix shows the split-affected stock within the DAX from 1-1-2004 to 10-31-2008.

The result of these calculation steps – the respective stock's average target price per month – is respectively shown within the tables for January 2004 until October 2008 in the column "Intrinsic value".[26]

II. Weighing of the respective stocks' intrinsic values:

With reference to the explanations of the DAX calculation in Section 6.3, the following formula describes how the DAX performance index is calculated:

---

[25] The arithmetical average of each stock's intrinsic value per month is shown in the excel sheet "DAX Performance Index - Intrinsic Value", Tab "2. Target Price per Month", located on the attached CD.
[26] The 58 tables for January 2004 until October 2008, are listed in the excel sheet "Performance Index - Intrinsic Value", Tab "3. Tables: Jan. 2004 - Nov. 2008" located on the attached CD.

$$Index_t = K_T * \frac{\sum_{i=1}^{n} p_{it} * q_{iT} * ff_{iT} * c_{it}}{\sum_{i=1}^{n} p_{io} * q_{io}} * Base .$$

Taking into consideration, that there should be calculated the intrinsic value of the DAX per month – instead of the actual price of the DAX – the price of stock i at time t (p_{it}) gets substituted by the average intrinsic value of stock i at time m (i_{im}). Assuming the other parameters are applied constantly – in analogy to the calculation of the actual price of the DAX – the intrinsic value of the DAX can be expressed by the formula:

$$Index_t = K_T * \frac{\sum_{i=1}^{n} i_{im} * q_{iT} * ff_{iT} * c_{it}}{\sum_{i=1}^{n} p_{io} * q_{io}} * Base .$$

The respective parameters necessary to be able to calculate the intrinsic value of the DAX refer to the last trading day of the month in consideration. They are based on the original data basis of the Deutsche Börse AG used for calculating the actual price of the DAX.[27] The intrinsic values of the DAX, for every of the 58 months, are shown within Tables 9 and 10 in the appendix.

Having successfully calculated the intrinsic value of the DAX, a comparison between the actual stock prices and the intrinsic values pursues the objective of being able to respond to the following two questions:

- How far do actual stock prices reflect their fundamentally justified values?
- How far fundamentally-driven analysis concepts are appropriate for being able to predict future stock price movements?

---

[27] The entire parameters for being able to calculate the intrinsic value of the Dax for each month, are listed within the 58 tables for January 2004 until October 2008. Those are listed in the excel-sheet "12-13-08 DAX Performance Index - Intrinsic Value", tab "3. Tables: Jan. 2004 - Nov. 2008" located on the attached CD.

With reference to these two questions, the following hypothesis can be formulated:

I. Actual DAX prices fluctuate around their intrinsic values. Consequently, the divergences between actual prices and intrinsic values could increase or decrease in the short run, but should decrease in the long run.

II. Considering a long time period of 58 months, there have to be periods during which actual DAX prices exceed their intrinsic value (particularly during booms) or during which actual DAX prices fall below their intrinsic value (particularly during crashes).

III. Assuming that actual DAX prices are mainly driven by fundamental factors, actual price trend reversals have to be the result of trend reversals in the intrinsic values. In addition to that, the strength of the intrinsic value trend reversal should indicate the approximate strength of the actual price reversal. Otherwise, it cannot be argued that the strength of price trend reversals is mainly determined by fundamental factors.

Figure 9 illustrates the actual prices of the DAX for each trading day (black line), compared with the average intrinsic value per month (red line). Arguing that the analysts' stock target prices try to predict the actual stock price movements within a period of six months, a second average intrinsic value per month has been drawn (green line) by simply time shifting the first moving average by six months into the future. It simply serves as an indication of whether the actual DAX prices have followed their intrinsic values.

The selection of noticeable time periods – during which the actual DAX price and its intrinsic value differ significantly – is restricted to six time periods from 1-1-2006 and 10-31-2008[28] (due to the higher number of analyst recommendations in comparison to the previous time period) so that the impact of randomly driven influencing factors on other conclusions is diminished as much as possible.

---

[28] First period: 5-3-2006 - 7-22-2006; second period: 11-18-2006 - 3-25-2007; third period: 4-24-2007 - 11-12-2007; fourth period: 11-27-2007 - 3-23-2008; fifth period: 5-3-2008 - 7-29-2008; sixth period: 8-23-2008 - 10-31-2008.

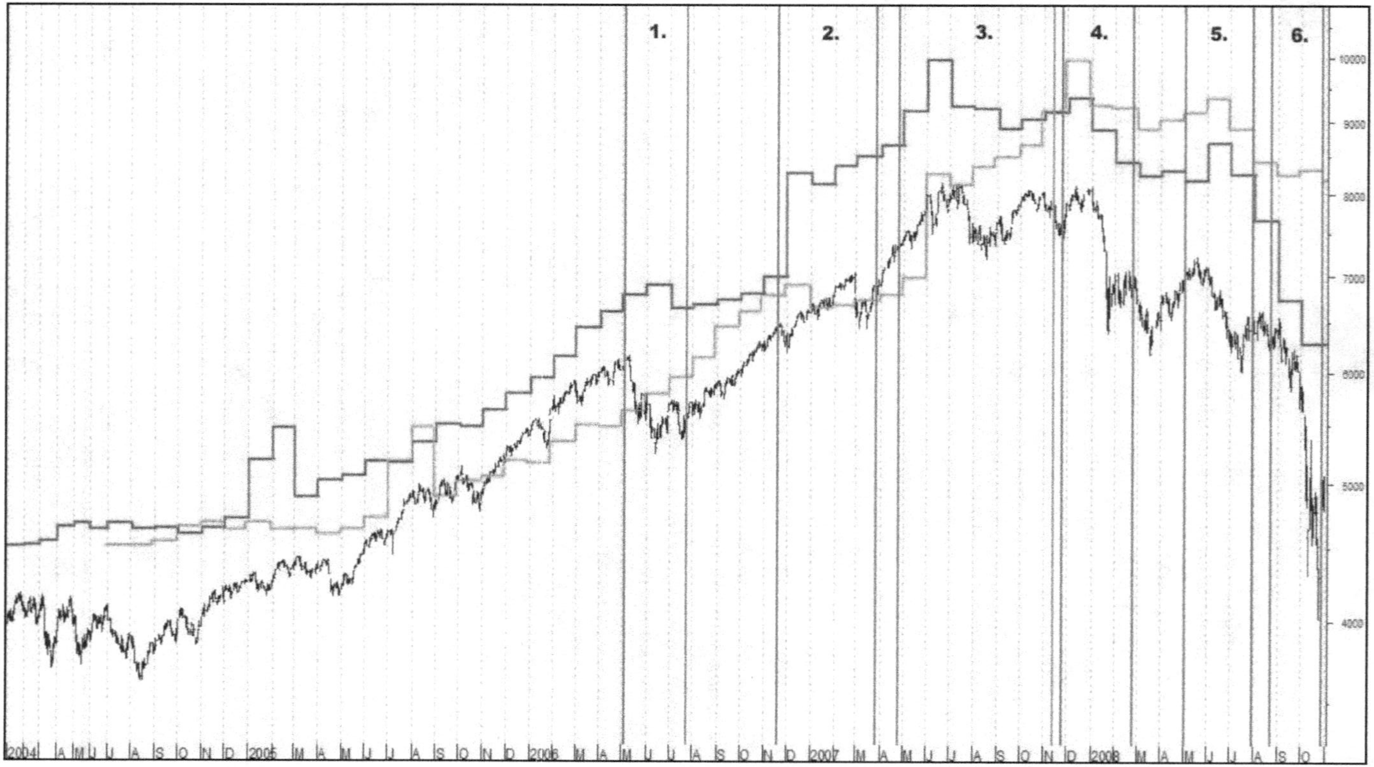

Figure 9: DAX Performance Index: Actual Prices versus Intrinsic Values

With reference to the previous formulated hypothesis, the following conclusions can be drawn by taking Figure 9 into consideration:

I. Actual DAX prices fluctuate around their intrinsic values. The divergences between actual prices and intrinsic values increase as well as decrease in the short run, but decrease in the long run. Nevertheless, you cannot state to which extent actual DAX prices follow their intrinsic values, due to the interpretation uncertainty, whether actual DAX prices follow their intrinsic values or vice versa. On the one hand, particularly the third, fourth and sixth time period show that actual prices follow their intrinsic values, at least to a certain degree. On the other hand, some time periods – documented by the first, second and fifth time period – indicate that intrinsic values also seem to follow actual prices. Nevertheless, we can conclude that there is a significant correlation between actual prices and intrinsic values.

II. During the entire period of 58 months, there has not been even one single time period during which actual DAX prices exceed their intrinsic value. Taking other empirical studies into consideration[29], this is a significant indication that fundamentally-driven equity analysts are not just driven by fundamental factors, but are subjected by behavioral irrationalities, leading to overoptimism.

III. Actual DAX price trend reversals are sometimes, but not always, indicated by intrinsic value trend reversals. Considering the third, fourth and sixth time periods, an intrinsic value trend reversal indicates an actual price trend reversal. In contrast to that, the first, second and fifth time period show that the intrinsic value trend reversal only occurs, after the actual DAX price trend reversal has already taken place.

Independent of which of the six time periods is considered, the concept of intrinsic value is not appropriate for determining the strength of crashes. This is a clear indication that fundamental factors are neglected during crashes, whereas psychological factors gain in impact.

---

[29] Barber et al. (2003) empirically proved equity analysts' recommendation to be permanently too optimistic. Henze (2004) confirms this result for the German stock market.

6.3.1.2. Sentiment Indicators

Having evaluated behavioral finance (see Chapter 4.), we can conclude that sentiment indicators (see Section 4.3.) are the only behavioral finance tool enabling investors to measure psychologically influencing factors quantitatively. Thus, sentiment indicators enable investors to draw conclusions to what extent actual stock prices are driven by psychological factors. Consequently, stock market phases of overreaction or underreaction can be recognized.

Assuming that phases of exaggeration indicate the reversal of a prevailing market trend – which is the basic assumption of the contrarian investment approach[30] – phases of overreaction or underreaction can be exploited for selling or buying stock.

With regard to the practical study, the DAX sentiment index[31] - as one of the most widely used sentiment indicators – is applied to the DAX, in order to be able to answer the following two questions:

- Is the DAX sentiment index appropriate to determine phases of overreaction or underreaction?

- Does the identification of phases of overreaction or underreaction enable investors to draw conclusion on the further stock market development?

---

[30] The contrarian investment approach encompasses all of the investment strategies that are characterized by making investments contrary to the majority of stock market investors (Dreman 1998, Montier 2007). Consequently, contrarian investment strategies are anticyclical investment strategies (Dressendörfer 1999). With the assumption that the majority of stock market participants agreed about the attractiveness of a stock, the majority of stock market participants would already have been invested in that stock, so that further demand for buying the stock is exhausted. Consequently, the stock is assumed to decrease in the future, due to the fact that supply will exceed demand (Cesar 1996).

[31] The Sentiment index is calculated by a weekly executed survey, asking the market participants about their expectation of the DAX development in the next six months. Four different answers are allowed: bullish, bearish, neutral, and no opinion.

On the basis of that survey, the Sentiment index can be calculated by the formula:

$Sentiment = \dfrac{bulls - bears}{votes}$. By putting the difference of bullish and bearish investors in relation to all votes, stock market phases of overreaction or underreaction are indicated.

Figure 10 shows the DAX sentiment index from 01-12-07 to 09-19-08:

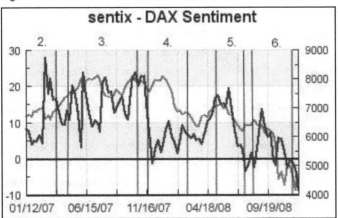

Figure 10: DAX Sentiment Index

The blue line shows the market participants' sentiment – calculated as the difference of bulls and bears divided by all votes of the survey –, whereas the gray line shows the actual stock price development of the DAX.

Referring to the concept of contrarian investment, local extreme values characterize phases of overreaction or underreaction, such that the prevailing market phase can be assumed to be more likely to reverse than to continue.

With regard to the previously determined six periods, during which actual prices diverged significantly from their intrinsic values (see Section 6.3.1.3.), all time periods - except for the first one - are examined by the DAX sentiment index in the following:

On the one hand, particularly the second, fifth and sixth time periods illustrate that the DAX decreased significantly, after the sentiment index has achieved a local maximum. Considering the fourth period, we can determine that the DAX slightly increased after the sentiment index achieved a local minimum. Nevertheless, the predictive capabilities of local minimums are not as good as those of local maximums. On the other hand, the fourth period indicates that there are stock market phases during which local extreme values of the sentiment index are not appropriate for predicting the future development of the DAX.

Taking the third period into consideration, two behavioral irrationalities of market participants are illustrated quantitatively by the sentiment index – the anchoring effect and the reference point effect (see Section 4.2.1.2.). During the third period, the DAX goes sideways, due to the fact that the former all-time high of 8'151.57 – achieved on July 13, 2007 – could not have been broken over the long run. Taking the anchoring effect into consideration, stock market participants' estimations about the DAX development during the next six months, are anchored to the former all-time high of 8'151.57 points. In addition to that, actual DAX prices also fail to break this all time high several times, due to the reference point effect. Gains are judged relative to the all-time high, so that the supply increasingly exceeds the demand, the nearer the DAX moves to its all-time high. Consequently, the DAX moves sideways instead of breaking its all time high.

All in all, the sentiment index can be considered to be appropriate for determining local extreme values during which stock market participants are too optimistic or pessimistic. Those phases of exaggeration can be used for selling or buying stock. Nevertheless, there are still stock market phases during which the sentiment index is not able to predict the future development of the DAX just by determining local extreme values.

6.3.1.3. Technical Indicators

Evaluating technical analysis (see Chapter 5.), the RSI (see Section 5.2.2.2.) as well as the MACD (see Section 5.2.2.1.) – being one of the most used technical indicators – are applied to the practical example of the DAX, in order to be able to answer the following question:

- Are technical indicators – represented by the RSI and the MACD – appropriate to time stock market investments?

In practice, RSI values over 70 indicate that a stock is overbought, whereas RSI values under 30 indicate that a stock is oversold. The MACD delivers trading signals by comparing the trend line (red line) with the signal line (black dashed line). If the trend line crosses the signal line from a downward swing to an upward swing, then a buy signal is generated, whereas a sell signal is generated, if the trend line crosses the signal line from the top heading downwards. In the following, those trading rules are examined for the six time periods during which the actual DAX prices significantly diverged from their intrinsic values (see Section 6.3.1.1.). Figure 11 shows the application of the RSI as well as the MACD to the DAX:

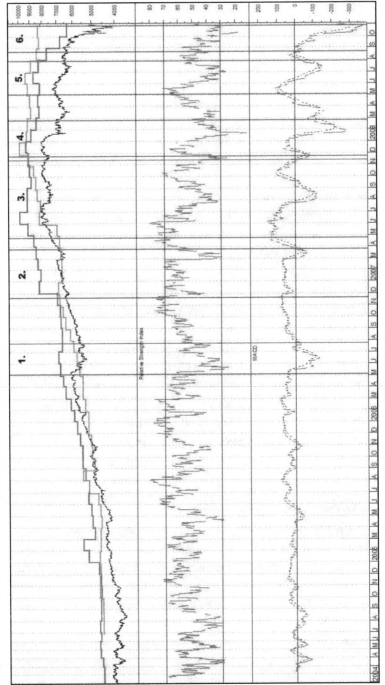

Figure 11: DAX Performance Index: Actual Prices versus RSI and MACD

On the one hand, the RSI as well as the MACD both generally generate too much buy and sell signals. As a result of that, investors would buy or sell stock too often, something that goes along with high transaction costs and non-optimally timed investment decisions.

On the other hand, decreasing or increasing stock markets were nevertheless indicated by the RSI and/or MACD, independent of the number of generated buy and sell signals, which was too high. The sudden stock market decreases during the first, second, fourth, fifth and sixth period were indicated by at least one of the indicators. During the second, fourth and fifth period, the RSI was near or even over its extreme value of 70. Consequently, decreasing stock markets were correctly indicated. During the first and the sixth period, the MACD's trend line crosses the signal line from the top downwards, so that a decreasing stock market was correctly indicated as well.

Increasing stock markets were correctly indicated by an RSI value near or even below 30 during all periods, except for the third period. With the exception of the sixth period, the RSI buy-signals were supported by the fact that the MACD's trend line crossed the signal line from the bottom upwards, which is a further indication of increasing stock markets. Nevertheless, the sideways trend of the third time period could not have been indicated by the RSI or the MACD.

Taking these results into consideration, we can determine that technical indicators are appropriate for giving at least an impression as to whether the prevailing trend will reverse. Nevertheless, technical indicators have their weaknesses in generating too many buy and sell signals, resulting in high transaction costs. Sub-optimally timed investment decisions are received, if buy and sell signals are not considered in the context of the results of further analysis methods.

6.3.2. Practical Synthesis Capabilities

The practical study of how far fundamental analysis (see Section 6.3.1.1.), sentiment indicators (see Section 6.3.1.2.) and technical indicators (see Section 6.3.1.3.) are able to predict the future stock price development of the DAX – by taking fundamental, psychological as well as timing aspects into consideration – leads us to the conclusion, that the theoretical strengths of each analysis concept can also be confirmed in practice.

Fundamental analysis is able to approximately calculate an intrinsic value that significantly correlates with the mid-term and long-term development of actual stock prices. Sentiment indicators are appropriate for making psychologically influencing factors measurable, whereas technical indicators give at least an indication for the short-term timing, when a stock should be bought or sold.

Taking the main assumptions about the theoretical synthesis capabilities of fundamental analysis, behavioral finance and technical analysis (see Section 6.2.) into consideration, we can determine that these can also be considered as proven in practice. For the mid-term and long-term, the DAX follows its intrinsic value, but there are at least two psychologically influencing factors that cannot be explained by fundamental analysis.

Firstly, the fundamentally-driven estimations about the intrinsic value of the DAX are permanently too optimistic. Consequently, fundamentally-driven evaluators could be psychologically coached in order to prevent such irrationalities in determining an intrinsic value.

Secondly, strongly decreasing stock markets are neither sufficiently indicated by fundamental analysis (only during the first, second and fifth period), nor is fundamental analysis capable of determining the extent of the correction (e.g. during the fourth and sixth period).

Therefore, the strengths of sentiment indicators as well as technical indicators are applied in practice. Sentiment indicators enable the investor to recognize phases during which the stock market participants are overoptimistic (second, fifth and sixth period) or too pessimistic (fourth period), so that the stock market is considered to be more likely to reverse than to continue.

In addition to that, potential areas of strong resistance (third period) – caused by psychological phenomena such as anchoring or the reference point effect – can be pointed out by sentiment indicators.

Technical indicators are appropriate to time the investment decision in the short term, but would generate two many trading signals, if they are applied without taking the results of the other two concepts into consideration.

The practical synthesis capabilities of the fundamental analysis, behavioral finance and technical analysis tend to become noticeable, if the second and third periods are to be used as an example:

During the second period, the intrinsic value is not able to indicate strongly decreasing stock prices, but the sentiment indicator has reached a local maximum. In addition to that, the RSI has reached values near to 70 and the MACD's trend line crosses its signal line from bottom to top. By just considering the intrinsic value, the prediction of decreasing stock prices would not have been possible, but by taking the respective strengths of the two further analysis concepts into consideration, the decrease becomes predictable.

During the third phase, neither the RSI nor the MACD were able to predict the DAX to move sideways. The trend reversal of the intrinsic value gives an indication that actual stock prices could start to decrease slightly. Taking into consideration that the sentiment indicator indicates, that the majority of the stock market participants do not assume the DAX to break its all time high of 8'151.57 points, actual stock prices can be assumed to be more likely to go sideways, than to break lastingly through the former all-time high.

6.4. Preliminary Conclusion

The theoretical (see Section 6.2.) as well as the practical (see Section 6.3.) examination of the synthesis capabilities of fundamental analysis, behavioral finance and technical analysis ultimately concludes that the three analysis concepts are able to supplement each other with their respective strengths.

Fundamental analysis has its strengths in calculating an intrinsic value, which enables investors to evaluate if actual stock prices reflect the fundamentally justified value of a company. Behavioral finance enables investors to become aware of what and to which extent actual stock prices are driven by psychologically influencing factors, so that phases of overreaction or underreaction can be determined. Technical analysis enables investors to time their investment decision in the short term, in order to prevent buying or selling a stock during unfavorable market phases.

The synthesis concept combines these strengths, so that the synthesis concept as a whole is less susceptible to changing influencing factors on the stock market. This is due to the fact, that some of the weaknesses of the respective analysis concept could have been successfully eliminated by combining the respective strengths. That was shown by evaluating the practical synthesis capabilities with the example of the DAX. Nevertheless, some threats for the predictive capability of the synthesis concept still remain and cannot be eliminated by combining the respective strengths – e.g. if the EMH or the semi-efficient form of information efficiency turn out to be permanently fulfilled on the stock market.

7. Final Conclusion and Outlook

The predictive capabilities of fundamental analysis, behavioral finance and technical analysis are dependent on the efficiency of the stock market. The examinations made in Chapter 2, have shown that the weak as well as the semi-strong forms of information efficiency are at least doubtful to be fulfilled on the stock market, whereas the strong efficiency form is clearly rejected. As such, the fulfillment of the EMH in any stock market phase is also at least questionable. Consequently, the fundamental analysis, behavioral finance and technical analysis cannot be judged to be generally worthless and are at least necessary to achieve a certain extent of information efficiency.

Considering the results detailed in Chapter 3, empirical studies have proven that actual stock market prices follow the respective company's intrinsic values in the long run, but can diverge on the short term, due to non-fundamental influencing factors. Therefore, the main premises of fundamental analysis are confirmed empirically.

Fundamental analysis has its strengths in enabling stock market investors to determine whether a stock should be fundamentally bought or sold, by comparing the intrinsic value with the actual stock market price. In addition to that, investors gain an impression with which, and to which extent, the company's intrinsic values are affected by different influencing factors. Nevertheless, the concept of fundamental analysis has weaknesses in that it can neither determine the precise point in time when a stock should be bought or sold, nor can it predict or explain non-fundamentally-driven stock price movements. Consequently, fundamental analysis could be improved in terms of concrete timing decisions as well as considering non-rational influencing factors.

Considering the results of Chapter 4, empirical studies have proven that stock markets are subjected by recurring anomalies. Those anomalies cannot be explained by concepts assuming stock market participants to act rationally, making it necessary for behavioral finance to supplement rationally-based analysis concepts with psychological and sociological cognitions. Behavioral finance has its strengths in enabling stock market investors to evaluate to what extent and by which factors stock market prices are actually driven by psychological influencing factors – particularly by the application of sentiment indicators that make psychological phenomena quantitatively measurable. Nevertheless, behavioral finance is neither able to determine a company's fair value, nor has the aggregation of qualitative cognitions for the separate behavioral finance theories come close to achieving an overall behavioral finance concept. Consequently behavioral finance has to be advanced in terms of its closeness to an overall behavioral concept as well as being able to determine a company's fair value.

Considering the results of Chapter 5, empirical studies proved that the stock market does not move randomly. Therefore, the main premises of technical analysis – predicting future stock price movements by analyzing historical stock prices – is comprehensible. Still, empirical studies have just proven that at least some technical indicator concepts enable stock market investors to generate an abnormal return in comparison to a simple buy-and-hold strategy, whereas chart analysis is not empirically verifiable. Technical analysis has its strengths in enabling investors to time their stock investments, but isn't scientifically proven. Consequently, technical analysis could be advanced by scientifically proven cognitions of behavioral finance as well as by acknowledging fundamentally-driven analysis concepts that are essential for achieving a certain extent of fundamental information efficiency on the stock market.

The theoretical as well as the practical examinations of the synthesis capabilities of fundamental analysis, behavioral finance and technical analysis lead to the conclusion that the three analysis concepts can supplement each other with their respective strengths. By combining these strengths, the synthesis concept as a whole is less susceptible towards changing influencing factors on the stock market. This is due to the fact, that some of the weaknesses of the respective analysis concept could have been successfully eliminated by combining the respective strengths. That can be seen by evaluating the practical synthesis capabilities by the DAX example. Nonetheless, some threats to the predictive capability of the synthesis concept still remain and cannot be eliminated by simply combining the respective strengths – e.g. if the EMH or the semi-efficient form of information efficiency turn out to be permanently fulfilled on the stock market. Taking the cognitions of the developed synthesis concept into consideration, further scientific and practical studies should be aimed towards improving the synthesis capabilities of fundamental analysis, behavioral finance and technical analysis (in detail) instead of continuing to consider these three concepts as being competitors. From the author's point of view, this would be an opportunity to improve the prevailing concepts for analyzing stock markets in the future.

Appendix

Stock	Stock Split Consideration	Stock Split Ratio
Adidas AG	6-19-2006	1:4
BASF SE	9-30-2008	1:2
Bayerische Hypo- und Vereinbank AG	6-21-2004	1'000:1'041
Deutsche Börse AG	6-15-2007	1:2
EON AG	9-30-2008	1:3
Fresenius Medical Care KGaA	9-28-2007	1:3
Henkel AG & Co. KGaA	9-28-2007	1:3
SAP AG	3-30-2007	1:4

Table 6: Stock Splits of DAX Performance Index Members during 1-1-2004 - 10-31-2008

Stock	Starting Date	Ending Date
Adidas AG	1-1-2004	10-31-2008
Allianz SE	1-1-2004	10-31-2008
Altana AG	1-1-2004	6-18-2007
BASF SE	1-1-2004	10-31-2008
Bayer AG	1-1-2004	10-31-2008
Bayerische Hypo- und Vereinbank AG	1-1-2004	12-19-2005
BMW AG	1-1-2004	10-31-2008
Commerzbank AG	1-1-2004	10-31-2008
Continental AG	1-1-2004	10-31-2008
Daimler AG	1-1-2004	10-31-2008
Deutsche Bank AG	1-1-2004	10-31-2008
Deutsche Börse AG	1-1-2004	10-31-2008
Deutsche Lufthansa AG	1-1-2004	10-31-2008
Deutsche Post AG	1-1-2004	10-31-2008
Deutsche Postbank AG	9-18-2006	10-31-2008
Deutsche Telekom AG	1-1-2004	10-31-2008
EON AG	1-1-2004	10-31-2008
Fresenius Medical Care KGaA	1-1-2004	10-31-2008
Henkel AG & Co. KGaA	1-1-2004	10-31-2008
Hypo Real Estate Holding AG	12-19-2005	10-31-2008
Infineon Technologies AG	1-1-2004	10-31-2008
K+S AG	9-22-2008	10-31-2008
Linde AG	1-1-2004	10-31-2008
MAN AG	1-1-2004	10-31-2008
Merck KGaA	6-18-2007	10-31-2008
Metro AG	1-1-2004	10-31-2008
Münchener Rückversicherungs-Gesellschaft AG	1-1-2004	10-31-2008
RWE AG	1-1-2004	10-31-2008
SAP AG	1-1-2004	10-31-2008
Schering AG	1-1-2004	9-18-2006
Siemens AG	1-1-2004	10-31-2008
ThyssenKrupp AG	1-1-2004	10-31-2008
TUI AG	1-1-2004	9-22-2008
Volkswagen AG	1-1-2004	10-31-2008

Table 7: Index Memberships of the DAX Performance Index during 1-1-2004 - 10-31-2008

Stock	Number of Analyst Recommendations	
	In Total	In Percentage
Adidas AG	407	3.27%
Allianz SE	482	3.87%
Altana AG	87	0.70%
BASF SE	370	2.97%
Bayer AG	635	5.10%
Bayerische Hypo- und Vereinbank AG	1	0.01%
BMW AG	482	3.87%
Commerzbank AG	329	2.64%
Continental AG	395	3.17%
Daimler AG	630	5.06%
Deutsche Bank AG	538	4.32%
Deutsche Börse AG	229	1.84%
Deutsche Lufthansa AG	327	2.62%
Deutsche Post AG	307	2.46%
Deutsche Postbank AG	225	1.81%
Deutsche Telekom AG	559	4.49%
EON AG	537	4.31%
Fresenius Medical Care KGaA	294	2.36%
Henkel AG & Co. KGaA	272	2.18%
Hypo Real Estate Holding AG	475	3.81%
Infineon Technologies AG	293	2.35%
K+S AG	17	0.14%
Linde AG	294	2.36%
MAN AG	240	1.93%
Merck KGaA	260	2.09%
Metro AG	509	4.08%
Münchener Rückversicherungs-Gesellschaft AG	431	3.46%
RWE AG	455	3.65%
SAP AG	644	5.17%
Schering AG	31	0.25%
Siemens AG	625	5.02%
ThyssenKrupp AG	372	2.99%
TUI AG	254	2.04%
Volkswagen AG	456	3.66%
Sum	**12'462**	**100%**

Table 8: Distribution of Analyst Recommendations Employed within the Empirical Study

Date	Intrinsic Value	Actual Price	Difference
Jan-04	4514.74	4058.60	456.14
Feb-04	4520.98	4018.16	502.82
Mar-04	4548.01	3856.70	691.31
Apr-04	4658.25	3985.21	673.05
May-04	4682.24	3921.41	760.82
Jun-04	4638.09	4052.73	585.35
Jul-04	4684.09	3895.61	788.47
Aug-04	4638.92	3785.21	853.71
Sep-04	4642.53	3892.90	749.63
Oct-04	4605.31	3960.25	645.07
Nov-04	4644.04	4126.00	518.04
Dec-04	4726.42	4256.08	470.34
Jan-05	5192.17	4245.36	946.82
Feb-05	5476.11	4350.49	1125.62
Mar-05	4892.21	4348.77	543.43
Apr-05	5016.08	4184.84	831.24
May-05	5061.18	4460.63	600.54
Jun-05	5188.28	4586.28	602.00
Jul-05	5171.62	4886.50	285.13
Aug-05	5348.15	4829.69	518.46
Sep-05	5500.21	5044.12	456.09
Oct-05	5485.47	4929.07	556.40
Nov-05	5638.27	5193.40	444.87
Dec-05	5789.91	5408.26	381.66
Jan-06	5949.72	5674.15	275.57
Feb-06	6147.69	5796.04	351.66
Mar-06	6458.11	5970.08	488.03
Apr-06	6618.61	6009.89	608.73
May-06	6791.34	5692.86	1098.47
Jun-06	6909.63	5683.31	1226.32
Jul-06	6659.03	5681.97	977.06
Aug-06	6681.32	5859.57	821.75
Sep-06	6743.82	6004.33	739.49
Oct-06	6805.90	6268.92	536.97
Nov-06	6990.40	6309.19	681.20
Dec-06	8280.47	6596.92	1683.55

Table 9: DAX Performance Index: Intrinsic Value versus Actual Prices (January 2004 - December 2006)

Date	Intrinsic Value	Actual Price	Difference
Jan-07	8126.12	6789.11	1337.01
Feb-07	8371.57	6715.44	1656.13
Mar-07	8496.39	6917.03	1579.36
Apr-07	8659.59	7408.87	1250.72
May-07	9160.65	7883.04	1277.60
Jun-07	9952.60	8007.32	1945.28
Jul-07	9240.74	7584.14	1656.60
Aug-07	9199.49	7638.17	1561.32
Sep-07	8889.84	7861.51	1028.33
Oct-07	9032.37	8019.22	1013.14
Nov-07	9138.14	7870.52	1267.62
Dec-07	9360.99	8067.32	1293.68
Jan-08	8878.07	6851.75	2026.32
Feb-08	8424.10	6748.13	1675.97
Mar-08	8249.40	6534.97	1714.42
Apr-08	8305.99	6948.82	1357.17
May-08	8180.93	7096.79	1084.14
Jun-08	8682.49	6418.32	2264.18
Jul-08	8259.10	6479.56	1779.54
Aug-08	7665.46	6422.30	1243.16
Sep-08	6739.37	5831.02	908.34
Oct-08	6292.14	4987.97	1304.17

Table 10: DAX Performance Index: Intrinsic Value versus Actual Prices (January 2007 - October 2008)

Bibliography

ABARBANELL, J. AND BERNHARD, 1992. Test of analysts' overreaction/underreaction to earnings information as an explanation for anomalous stock price behaviour, The Journal of Finance, 47, 1181-1207.

ACHELIS, S.B., 1995. *Technical Analysis from A to Z.* Chicago: Irwin.

ADERS, C., GALLI, A. AND WIEDEMANN F., 2000. Unternehmenswerte auf Basis der Multiplikatormethode? – Eine Überprüfung mit dem Netto-Ansatz der DCF-Methode. Finanz Betrieb, 4, 197-204.

ALBRECHT, P. AND MAURER, R., 2005. *Investment- und Risikomanagement.* 2nd ed. Stuttgart: Schäffer-Poeschel.

ALEXANDER, S. 1961. Price Movements in Speculative Markets: Trends or Random Walks. Industrial Management Review, 2 (2), 7-26.

ALEXANDER, S. 1964. Price Movements in Speculative Markets: Trends or Random Walks. Industrial Management Review, 5 (2), 25-46.

ALIBER, R.Z. AND KINDLEBERGER, C.P., 2005. *Manias, Panics and Crashes – A History of Financial Crises.* 5th ed. New Work: John Wiley & Sons.

ALLEN, F., BREALY, R.A. AND MYERS S.C., 2006. *Corporate Finance.* 8th ed. New York: McGraw-Hill.

AMIR, E. AND GANZACH, Y., 1998. Overreaction and underreaction in analysts' forecasts. Journal of Economic Behavior & Organization, 37 (3), 333-347.

ANDREASSEN, P.B., 1990. Judgemental Extrapolation and Market Overreaction: On the Use and Disuse of News. Journal of Behavioral Decision Making, 3, 153-174.

ANTIKAROV, V., COPELAND, C. AND COPELAND, T.E., 2003. *Real Options: A Practitioner's Guide.* London: Texere.

ANTONIOU, A., LAM, H. AND KRISHNA, P., 2007. Profitability of momentum strategies in international markets: The role of business cycle variables and behavioural biases. Journal of banking, 31 (3), 955-972.

ARONSON, D., 2007. Evidence-Based Technical Analysis – Applying the Scientific Method and Statistical Interference to Trading Signals. New York: John Wiley & Sons.

AUGE-DICKHUT, S. AND MOSER U., 2003. Unternehmensbewertung: Zum Zusammenhang zwischen Vergleichsverfahren und dem DCF-Verfahren. Finanz Betrieb, 4, 213-223.

BALL, R., 1978. Anomalies in Relationship Between Securities' Yield and Yield Surrogates. Journal of Financial Economics, 6, 103-126.

BALLWIESER, W., 1995. Aktuelle Aspekte der Unternehmensbewertung. Die Wirtschaftsprüfung, 51, 81-92.

BALLWIESER, W., 2007. Unternehmensbewertung – Prozess, Methoden, Probleme. Stuttgart: Schäffer-Poeschel.

BARBER, B., LEHAVY, R., MC NICHOLS M. AND TRUEMAN, B., 2003. Reassessing the Returns to Analysts' Stock Recommendations. Financial Analyst Journal, 59 (2), 88-96.

BARBERIS, N., SHLEIFER, A. AND VISHNY, R., 1998. A model of investor sentiement. Journal of Financial Economics, 49, 307-343.

BARTON, D., NEWELL, R. AND WILSON, G., 2003. Dangerous Markets – Managing in Financial Crises. New York: John Wiley & Sons.

BASSETTI, W.H.C., EDWARDS, R.D., MAGEE J., 2007. Technical Analysis of Stock Trends. 9th ed. Boca Raton: CRC Press.

BAUSCH, A., 2000. Die Multiplikatormethode – Ein betriebswirtschaftlich sinnvolles Instrument zur Unternehmens- und Kaufpreisfindung in Akquisitionsprozessen? Finanz Betrieb, 7-8, 448-459.

BECKMANN, J., 1984. *Kognitive Dissonanz. Eine Handlungstheoretische Perspektive.* Berlin: Springer.

BECKMANN, C., KRONMÜLLER, A. AND PEEMÖLLER V.H., 2002. Empirische Erhebung zum aktuellen Stand der praktischen Anwendung des Realoptionsansatzes. Finanz Betrieb, 4 (10), S. 561-565.

BEHAVIOURAL FINANCE GROUP, 1999. Behavioural Finance – Idee und Überblick. In: M. WEBER, ed. Behavioral Finance Group – Forschung für die Praxis. Mannheim: Lehrstuhl für ABWL, Finanzwirtschaft insbesondere Bankbetriebslehre University of Mannheim, Volume 0.

BEHRINGER, S., 2007. *Cash-flow und Unternehmensbeurteilung – Berechnungen und Anwendungsfelder für die Finanzanalyse.* 9th ed. Berlin: Erich Schmidt Verlag.

BEIKE, R. AND SCHLÜTZ, J., 2005. *Finanznachrichten: Lesen – verstehen – nutzen – Ein Wegweiser durch Kursnotierungen und Marktberichte.* 4th ed. Stuttgart: Schäffer-Poeschel.

BEKAERT, G., ERB, C., HARVEY, C. AND VISKANTA, T., 1997. What Matters for Emerging Equity Market Investments. Emerging Markets Quarterly, 2, 17-46.

BERGOLD, U. AND MAYER B., 2005. *Markt und Meinung – Mit Behavioral Finance und Technische Analyse zu den Gewinnern gehören.* Munich: FinanzBuch Verlag.

BERRY T.D. AND HOWE K. M., 1994. Public Information Arrival. The Journal of Finance, 49, 1331-1346.

BERRY, M. AND DREMAN, D., 1995. Overreaction, Underreaction and the Low P/E Effect. Financial Analysts Journal, 51, 21-30.

BERTONECHE, M. L., 1979. Spectral Analysis of Stock Market Prices. Journal of Banking and Finance, 3, 210-218.

BERTRAM, S. AND HAAS, A., 2008. Medien und Aktien – Theoretische und emprisiche Modellierung der Rolle der Berichterstattung für das Börsengeschehen. Wiesbaden: VS Verlag.

BIKHCHANDANI, S., HIRSHLEIFER, D. AND WELCH I., 1998. Learning form the Behavior of Others: Conformity, Fads, and Informational Cascades. Journal of Economic Perspectives, 12 (3), 151-170.

BINSWANGER, M., 2004. How important are fundamentals – Evidence from structural VAR model for the stock markets in the US, Japan and Europe. Journal of international financial markets, institutions & money, 14 (2), 185-201.

BLUME M.E. AND FAMA, E.F., 1966. Filter Rules and Stock-Market Trading. Journal of Business, 39, 226-241.

BOHL, M.T. AND SIKLOS P.L., 2001. Detecting Speculative Bubbles in Stock Prices: A New Approach and Some Evidence for the US. Frankfurt am Main: Deutsche Bank.

BÖMELBURG, P., DENKMANN A. AND PEEMÖLLER, V., 1994. Unternehmensbewertung in Deutschland. Die Wirtschaftsprüfung, 47, 741-749.

BOROWICZ, F., 2005. Methoden der Unternehmensbewertung – Ertragswertmethode, Discounted Cash Flow und Economic Value Added. Wirtschaftswissenschaftliches Studium, 7, 368-373.

BREUER, W., 2008. Bounded Rationality, Rights Offerings, and Optimal Subscription Prices. Schmalenbach Business Review, 7, 224-248.

BRIGHAM, E.F. AND HOUSTON J. F., 1998. Fundamentals of Financial Management. 8th ed. Mason: South-Western.

BROCK, J., 1994. International Anlagestrategie – Rationale Entscheidung durch technische Analyse. Thesis (PhD). University of Marburg.

BROCK, W., LAKONISHOK, J. AND LEBARON, B., 1992. Simple Technical Trading Rules and the Stochastic Properties of Stock Returns. The Journal of Finance, 47, 1731-1764.

BROMANN, O., SCHIERECK, D. AND WEBER, M., 1997. Reichtum durch (anti-)zyklische Handelsstrategien am deutschen Aktienmarkt? Zeitschrift für betriebswirtschaftliche Forschung, 49, 603-616.

BRÖSEL, G. AND MATSCHKE M., 2007. Unternehmensbewertung. Funktionen – Methoden – Grundsätze. 3rd ed. Wiesbaden: Gabler.

BROWN, K.C., 1999. Technical Analysis for the Trading Professionals – Strategies and Techniques for Today's Turbulent Financial Markets. New York: McGraw-Hill.

BROWN, K.C. AND REILLY F.K., 2006. Investment Analysis and Portfolio Management. 8th ed. Mason: Thomson Higher Education.

BRUNNERMEIER, M.K., 2001. Asset Pricing under Asymmetric Information – Bubbles, Crashes, Technical Analysis and Herding. Oxford: Oxford University Press.

BRUNS, C. AND STEINER M., 2007. Wertpapiermanagement – Professionelle Wertpapieranalyse und Portfoliostrukturierung. 9th ed. Stuttgart: Schaeffer-Poechel Verlag.

BULKOWSKI, T.N., 2006. Enzyklopädie der Chart Muster – Chartformationen erkennen und verstehen. 2nd ed. Munich: FinanzBuch Verlag.

BUSKAMP, F.J., 2004. Mentale Börsenkompetenz – Investieren mit Fingerspitzengefühl. Munich: FinanzBuch Verlag.

CAMERER, C. AND WEBER M., 1991. The Disposition Effect in Securities Trading: An Experimental Analysis. Working Paper: University of Kiel.

CAMERER, C. AND WEBER, M., 1998. The Disposition Effect in Securities Trading: An Experimental Analysis. Journal of Economic Behavior & Organization, 33 (2), 167-184.

CAMPELL, J.Y. AND SHILLER R.J., 1988a. Stock Prices, Earnings, and Expected Dividends. The Journal of Finance, 43 (3), 661-676.

CAMPBELL, J.Y. AND SHILLER R.J., 1988b. The dividend-price ratio and expectations of future dividends and discount factors. Review of Financial Studies, 1, 195-228.

CESAR, G., 1996. Aktienanalyse heute – Gewinnmaximierung an der Börse. Wiesbaden: Gabler Verlag.

CHAN, K., JEGADEESH, N. AND LAKONISHOK, 1996. Momentum Strategies. The Journal of Finance, 51, 1681-1713.

CHAN, K., HAMEED, A. AND TONG, W., 2000. Profitability of Momentum Strategies in the International Equity Markets. Journal of financial and quantitative analysis, 35 (2), 153-172.

CHUNG, H. AND LEE, B.S., 1998. Fundamental and non-fundamental components in stock price of Pacific-Rim countries. The Journal of Finance, 6, 321-346.

COENENBERG A. G. AND SCHULTZE, W., 2002. Das Multiplikator-Verfahren in der Unternehmensbewertung: Konzeption und Kritik. Finanz Betrieb, 12, 697-703.

COLBY, R.W. AND MEYERS T.A., 2002. The Encyclopedia of Technical Market Indicators. 2nd ed. New York: Mc Graw Hill.

CONRAD, J. AND KAUL, G., 1988. Time-Variation in Expected Returns. Jorunal of Business, 61, 409-425.

COPELAND, T.E., KOLLER T. AND MURRIN J., 2002. *Unternehmenswert – Methoden und Strategien für eine wertorientierte Unternehmensführung.* 3rd ed. Frankfurt: Campus Verlag.

COVEL, M. 2004. *Trend Following – How Great Traders Make Millions in Up or Down Markets.* New Jersey: Prentice-Hall.

CRASSELT, N. AND TOMASZEWSKI, C., 1999. Realoptionen – Eine neue Methode der Investistionsrechnung? Wirtschaftswissenschaftliches Studium, 28, 556-559.

CUTHBERTSON, K. AND HYDE S., 2002. Excess volatility and efficiency in French and German stock markets. Economic modelling, 19 (2), 399-418.

DAHLQUIST, J.R. AND KIRKPATRICK C.D., 2007. *Technical Analysis – The Complete Resource for Financial Technicians.* New Jersey: Person Education.

DANGEL, T., DOCKNER, E.J., GAUNERSDORFER, A., PFISTER, A., SÖGNER, L. AND STROBEL, G., 2001. Adaptive Erwartungsbildung und Finanzmarktdynamik. Zeitschrift für betriebswirtschaftliche Forschung, June, 339-365.

DANIEL, K.D, HIRSHLEIFER, D. AND SUBRAHMANYAM, A., 2001. Overconfidence, Arbitrage, and Equilibrium Asset Pricing. The Journal of Finance, 56 (3), 921-965.

DAMODARAN, A., 2001. *The Dark Side of Valuation – Valuing Old Tech, New Tech, and New Economy Companies.* New York: Prentice Hall.

DAMODARAN, A., 2002. *Investment Valuation – Tools and Techniques for Determinig the Value of Any Asset.* 2nd ed. New York: John Wiley & Sons.

DAMODARAN, A., 2006. *Damodaran on Valuation – Security Analysis for Investment and Corporate Finance.* New Jersey: John Wiley & Sons.

DE BOND, W.F.M. AND THALER, R., 1985. Does the Stock Market Overreact? The Journal of Finance, 40 (3), 793-805.

DE BONDT, W.F.M. AND THALER, R., 1987. Further evidence on investor overreaction and stock market seasonality. The Journal of Finance, 42, 557-581.

DE BONDT, W.F.M. AND THALER R.H., 1995. Financial Decision-Making in Markets and Firms. In: R. Jarrow et al., ed. Handbocks in OR & MS. Amsterdam: Elsevier Science, 385-410.

DE BONDT, W.F.M. AND BRAV A., 2002. Discussion of "Competing Theories of Financial Anomalies." The Review of Financial Studies, 15 (2), 607-613.

DE FUSCO, R.A., MCLEAVY, D.W., PINTO, J.E. AND RUNKLE D.E., 2001. Quantitative Methods for Investment Analysis. Charlottesville: AIMR.

DE GRAUWE, P. AND GRIMALDI, M., 2004. Bubbles and Crashes in a Behavioral Finance Model. Munich: CESifo.

DEHMEL, I. AND HOMMEL M., 2008. Unternehmensbewertung case by case. 3rd ed. Frankfurt am Main: Verlag Recht und Wirtschaft.

DETER, H., DIEGELMANN, M., ROLF, M., SCHÖMIG, P.N. AND WIEHLE, U., 2005a. Unternehmensbewertung – Methoden, Rechenbeispiele, Vor- und Nachteile. 2nd ed. Wiesbaden: Cometis.

DETER, H., DIEGELMANN, M., ROLF, M., SCHÖMIG, P.N. AND WIEHLE, U., 2005b. 100 Finanzkennzahlen. Wiesbaden: Cometis.

DEUTSCHE BÖRSE AG, 2008. Short Information to the Equity- and Strategy Indices of Deutsche Börse – Version 2.4. Frankfurt on the Main: Deutsche Börse AG.

DORNBUSCH, D., 1998. Untersuchung von Modellen der Fundamentalen und Technischen Aktienanalyse – Ein empirischer Vergleich am deutschen Aktienmarkt. Thesis (PhD). RWTH Aachen University.

DREMAN, D., 1998. *Contrarian Investment Strategies: The Next Generation – Beat the Market by Goning Against the Crowd.* New York: Simon & Schuster.

DRESSENDÖRFER, J.M., 1999. Zyklische und antizyklische Investmentstrategien: theoretische Fundierung und empirische Überprüfung am Schweizer Aktienmarkt. Thesis (PhD). University of St. Gallen.

DRUKARCZYK, J. AND SCHÜLER, A., 2007. *Unternehmensbewertung.* 5th ed. München: Verlag Franz Vahlen.

DÜCK-RATH M., 2005. Unternehmensbewertung mit Hilfe von DCF-Methoden und ausgewählten Realoptionsansätzen. Thesis (PhD). University of Hamburg.

EASTON, P.D., 1985. Accouting Earnings and Security Valuation: Empirical Evidence of the Fundamental Links. Journal of Accounting Research, 23, 54-77.

EL-ERIAN, M., 2008. *When Markets Collide – Investment Strategies for the Age of Global Economic Change.* New York: Mc-Graw-Hill.

ELLENRIEDER, R., 2001. Synergetische Kapitalmarktmodelle – Erklärung der Wertpapierentwicklung durch Integration des menschlichen Anlegerverhaltens in einem Kapitalmarktmodell. Thesis (PhD). University of Augsburg.

FAIRFELD, P.M., 1994. P/E, P/B and the Present Value of Future Dividends. Financial Analysts Journal, 50 (7), 23-31.

FAMA, E.F., 1970. Efficient Capital Markets: A Review of Theory and Empirical Work. The Journal of Finance, 25 (2), 383-417.

FAMA, E.F., 1991. Efficient Capital Markets II, The Journal of Finance, 46 (5), 1575-1617.

FAMA, E.F. AND FRENCH, K.R., 1992. The Cross-Section of Expected Stock Returns. The Journal of Finance, 47 (2), 427-465.

FERRIS, S.P., HAUGEN, R.A. AND MAKHIJA, A.K., 1988. Predicting Contemporary Volume with Historic Volume at Differential Price Levels: Evidence Supporting the Disposition Effect. The Journal of Finance, 43, 677-697.

FIELLITZ, B.D. AND GREENE, M.T., 1977. Long-Term Dependence in Common Stock Returns. Journal of Financial Economics, 4, 339-349.

FINANCIAL TIMES, 2008a. Wave of profit warnings expected. Financial Times, 27. October, p.1.

FINANCIAL TIMES, 2008b. Take care not to be misled on when to call the bottom. Financial Times, 27. October, p.7.

FINANCIAL TIMES, 2008c. Porsche Intentions baffle markets – Hedge funds scramble to assess damage. Financial Times, 30. October, p.14.

FINANCIAL TIMES, 2008d. What's now 'In' should be 'Out'. Financial Times, 3. November, p.18.

FLEISCHER, K., 1999. Die Untauglichkeit des KGV zur Prognose von Aktienkursveränderungen. Zeitschrift für Betriebswirtschaft, 69 (1), 71-82.

FLEING, J., 2003. "Erkenne dich selbst und analysiere die Trends". Smart Investor, 6, 25-26.

FLOREK, E., 2000. Neue Trading Dimensionen – Nutzen Sie das Erfolgspotenzial modernster Börsen-Techniken. Munich: FinanzBuch Verlag.

FRANKE, G. AND HAX, H., 2003. Finanzwirtschaft des Unternehmens und Kapitalmarkt. 5th ed. Berlin: Springer.

FRANKFURTER, G.M., 2007. Market Efficiency cum Anomalies, or Behavioral Finance?, Homo Oeconomicus, 24 (1), 81-93.

FRENCH K. AND POTERBA J.M., 1991. Investor Diversification and International Equity Markets. American Economic Review, 81, 222-226.

GANTENBEIN, P. AND SPREMANN, K., 2005. *Kapitalmärkte*. Stuttgart: Lucius & Lucius.

GANTENBEIN, P. AND GEHRIG M., 2007. Moderne Unternehmensbewertung – Bewertungsziel mit Methodenmix erreichen. Der Schweizer Treuhänder, 9, 602-612.

GOLDBERG, J. AND VON NITZSCH R., 2000. *Behavioral Finance – Gewinnen mit Kompetenz*. 2nd ed. Munich: FinanzBuch Verlag.

GONEDES, N.J., 1976. The capital market, the market for information and external accounting. The Journal of Finance, 31, 611-630.

GOTHEIN, W., 1995. Evaluation von Anlagestrategien – Realisierung eines objektorientierten Simulators. Thesis (PhD). University of Heidelberg.

GRAHAM, J.R., 1999. Herding among Investment Newsletters: Theory and Evidence. The Journal of Finance, 54 (1), 237-268.

GRANGER, C.W. AND MORGENSTERN, O. 1970, Predictability of Stock Market Prices. Lexington: D.C. Heath and Company.

GRINBLATT, M., TITMAN, S. AND WERMERS, R., 1995. Momentum Strategies, Portfolio Performance, and Herding: A Study of Mutual Fund Behavior. American Economic Review, 85, 1088-1105.

GROSSMANN, S. AND STIGLITZ, J.E., 1980. On the Impossibility of Informationally Efficient Markets, The American Economic Review, 70 (3), 393-408.

HACHMEISTER, D., 1994. Der Discounted Cash Flow als Maß der Unternehmenswertsteigerung. Thesis (PhD). University of Munich.

HAUGEN, R.A., 1999. *The New Finance – The Case Against Efficient Markets.* 2nd ed. New Jersey: Prentice Hall.

HEILMAN, K., LAGER, V. AND OEHLER, A., 2000. The Disposition Effect in Experimental Call Markets. Working Paper. University of Bamberg.

HELBLING, C., 2007. Unternehmensbewertung im Wandel – Langfristige Entwicklungen auf dem Gebiet der Unternehmenbewertung. Der Schweizer Treuhänder, 6-7, 607-613.

HENZE, J., LUDWIG, B. AND RÖDER, K., 2003. Der Overconfidence Bias als eine Ursache für den Winner's Curse. Finanz Betrieb, 7-8, 468-472.

HENZE, J., 2004. Was leisten Finanzanalysten? – Eine empirische Analyse des deutschen Aktienmarktes. Thesis (PhD). University of Stuttgart.

HENSELMANN, K., 2002. Das Mischen von Unternehmenswerten – Replik zur Erwiderung von Kruschwitz/Lähm/Jahn, FB 2002 S. 145-148. Finanz Betrieb, 3, 149-157.

HERRMANN, A., MAINZ, F.H. AND WRICKE, M., 2000. Behavioral Pricining – Erklärungs- und Operationalisierungsansätze des Referenzpreiskonzepts. Wirtschaftswissenschaftliches Studium, 12, 692-697.

HILLERS, J., KUNOWSKI, S. AND PEEMÖLLER V., 1999. Ermittlung des Kapitalisierungszinssatzes für internationale Mergers and Acquisitions bei Anwendung des Discounted Cash Flow-Verfahrens (Entity-Ansatz). Eine empirische Erhebung. Die Wirtschaftsprüfung, 52, 621-630.

HOFFMANN, C., 2001. Gleichgerichtetes Verhalten am Aktienmarkt – Eine Verbindung ökonomischer, psychologischer und soziologischer Ansätze. Thesis (PhD). University of Cologne.

HOKE, M. 2002. Unternehmensbewertung auf Basis EVA – Erfahrungen bei der Implementierung eines EVA-basierten Bewertungsmodells. Der Schweizer Treuhänder, 9, 765-770.

HOLFORT, T., NELLES, M. AND UZIK, M., 2007. Rollierende Momentum-Strategien am deutschen Aktienmarkt. Finanz Betrieb, 7-8, 444-449.

HOMMEL, U. AND PRITSCH, G., 1999. Marktorientierte Investitionsbewertung mit dem Realoptionsansatz: Ein Implementierungsleitfaden für die Praxis. Finanzmarkt und Portfoliomanagement, 13, 121-141.

HOTZ, P., 2005. Das Anlagekonzept Behavioral Finance ist auf dem Prüfstand – Systematisch kann nicht prognostiziert werden – Diversifikation anstreben – Lohnt sich das Ausnutzen von Marktanomalien? Finanz und Wirtschaft, 13 July, p.20.

HRUBY, P.W., 1991. Kritische Betrachtung der Chart-Analyse. Thesis (PhD). University of Erlangen-Nuremberg.

HUBER, J., KIRCHLER, M. AND SUTTER M., 2006. Vom Nutzen zusätzlicher Information auf Märkten mit unterschiedlich informierten Händlern – Eine experimentelle Studie. Zeitschrift für betriebswirtschaftliche Forschung, March, 188-211.

HÜBNER, M. 2003. Sentimentanalyse mit dem sentix. Smart Investor, 6, 20-21.

HÜBNER, M. AND HUSSY, P., 2006. Behavioral Finance – sentix als Bindeglied zwischen Theorie und Praxis. Smart Investor, 9, 14-19.

IDW, 2007. *Entwurf einer Neufassung des IDW Standards: Grundsätze zur Durchführung von Unternehmensbewertungen.* Duesseldorf: IDW.

IKENBERRY, D., LAKONISHOK, J. AND VERMAELEN, T. (1995). Market Underreaction to Open Market Share Repurchases. Journal of Financial Economics, 39, 181-208.

JEGADEESH, N. AND TITMAN, S., 1993. Returns to buying winners and selling losers: implications for stock market efficiency. The Journal of Finance, 48, 65-91.

JÜNEMANN, B. AND SCHELLENBERGER, D., 1997. Investmentpsychologie – Ein modernes Konzept. Die Bank, 9, 562-565.

KAHNEMAN, D. AND TVERSKEY, A., 1979. Prospect Theory. An Analysis of Decision under Risk. Econometrica, 47, 263-291.

KAHNEMAN, D. AND TVERSKY, A., 1981. The Framing of Decisions and the Psychology of Choices. Science, 22, 453-458.

KAHNEMAN, D. AND TVERSKY A., 2000. Choices, Values and Frames. Cambridge: Cambridge University Press.

KAMES, C., 1999. Unternehmensbewertung durch Finanzanalysten als Ausgangspunkt eines value based measurement. Thesis (PhD): University of Passau.

KASPERZAK, R. AND KRAG J., 2007. Grundzüge der Unternehmensbewertung. 2nd ed. Munich: Beck.

KAUFMAN, P.J., 1998. Trading Systems and Methods. 3rd ed. New York: John Wiley & Sons.

KIEHLING, H., 2001. Börsenpsychologie und Behavioral Finance – Wahrnehmung und Verhalten am Aktienmarkt. Munich: Vahlen.

KIEHLING, H., 2008. Vom Behavioral Finance zur Econophysik. Die Bank, 4, 22-25.

KINNEY, W.R. AND ROZEFF, M.S., 1976. Capital Market Seasonality: The Case of Stock Returns. Journal of Financial Economics, 3, 379-402.

KOSFELD, R., 1996. *Kapitalmarketmodelle und Aktienbewertung. Eine statistische-ökonometrische Analyse.* Wiesbaden: Gabler.

KROLLE, S., 2001. Unsicherer tax shield in der Unternehmensbewertung – Adjusted Present Value (APV) oder Discounted Cash-flow (DCF). Finanz Betrieb, 1, 18-30.

KROLLE, S., SCHMITT, G. AND SCHWETZLER, B., 2005. *Multiplikatorverfahren in der Unternehmensbewertung – Anwendungsbereiche, Problemfälle, Lösungsalternativen.* Stuttgart: Schäffer-Poechel Verlag.

KRUSCHWITZ L. AND LÖFFLER A., 2003. Fünf typische Missverständnisse im Zusammenhang mit dem DCF-Verfahren. Finanz Betrieb, 11, 731-735.

LAKONISHOK, J., SHLEIFER, A. AND VISHNY, R., 1992. The impact of institutional trading on stock prices. Journal of Financial Economics, 32, 23-44.

LAKONISHOK, J., SHLEIFER A. AND VISHNY R., 1994. Contrarian investment, extrapolation, and risk. The Journal of Finance, 49, 1541-1578.

LANGER, E.J., 1975. The Illusion of Control. Journal of Personality and Social Psychology, 32, 311-328.

LASCHKE, A., 1999. Overconfidence – Schätzen Anleger ihre Kenntnisse falsch ein? In: M. WEBER, ed. Behavioral Finance Group – Forschung für die Praxis. Mannheim: Lehrstuhl für ABWL, Finanzwirtschaft insbesondere Bankbetriebslehre University of Mannheim, Volume 2.

LASER, J., 1995. Marktpsychologie und Börsentrends – Der Börsenzyklus unter psychologischen Aspekten. In: F. SCHMIELEWSKI, ed. Am Puls der Märkte – Moderne und bewährte Methoden der Kursdiagnostik. Frankfurt: Campus Verlag VTAD, 9-30.

LAWRENCE, E.R., MCCABE, G. AND PRAKASH, A.J., 2007. Answering Financial Anomalies: Sentiment-Based Stock Pricing. The Journal of Behavioral Finance, 8 (3), 161-171.

LEE, B.S., 1995. Fundamentals and bubbles in asset prices: Evidence from the US and Japanese asset prices. Financial Engineering and Japanese Financial Markets, 2, 69-122.

LEE, B.S., 1998. Permanent, temporary and non-fundamental components of stock prices. Journal of Financial and Qualitative Analysis, 33, 1-32.

LEROY, S. AND PORTER, R.D., 1981. The Present-Value: Tests Based on Implied Variance Bounds. Econometrica, 49, 555-574.

LINDNER, W. AND MÜLLER T., 2007. Das grosse Buch der Technischen Indikatoren – Alles über Oszillatoren, Trendfolger, Zyklentechnik. 9th ed. Rosenheim: TM Börsenverlag.

LO, A. W. AND MACKINLAY, A.C., 1988. Stock Market Prices Do Not Follow Random Walks: Evidence from a Simple Specification Test. Review of Financial Studies, 1, 41-66.

LO, A.W. AND MACKINLAY, A.C., 1999. A Non-Random Walk Down Wall Street. New Jersey: Princeton University Press.

LOHRBACH, T. AND SCHUMANN M., 1995. Aktienkurprognose mit technischen Indikatoren. Die Bank, 10, 617-621.

LOUGHRAN, T. AND RITTER J., 1996. Long-Term Market Overreaction: The Effect of Low-Priced Stocks. The Journal of Finance, 51, 1959-1970.

MAAS, P. AND WEIBLER J., 1997. Immer unter Spannung – Crash Konstellationen: Kontrollillusionen und Stress an der Börse. In: B. JÜNEMANN AND D. SCHELLENBERG, ed. Psychologie für Börsenprofis. Stuttgart: Schäffer-Poeschel, 109-122.

MALKIEL, B.G., 1999. *A Random Walk Down Wall Street.* New York: W.W. Norton & Company.

MATTERN, C., 2005. *Fundamentalanalyse im Portfoliomangement – Konjunkturindikatoren verstehen und analysieren.* Stuttgart: Schäffer-Poechel Verlag.

MCLEAVY, D., AND SOLNIK, B., 2003. *International Investments.* 5th ed. New York: Pearson Addison Wesley.

MENZ, K.M., 2004. Die Technische Analyse als Simplifikation des datengenerierenden Prozesses. Kreditwesen, 12, 627-630.

MEULBROEK, L.K., 1992. An Empirical Analysis of Illegal Insider Trading, The Journal of Finance, 47, 1661-1699.

MICHAELY, R., THALER, R.H. AND WOMACK K., 1995. Price Reactions to Dividend Initiations and Omissions: Overreaction or Drift? The Journal of Finance, 50, 573-608.

MILLER, G.A., 1956. The Magical Number Seven, Plus or Minor Two: Some Limits on our Capacity for Processing Information. Psychological Review, 63, 81-97.

MÖLLER, H.P., 1985. Die Informationseffizienz des deutschen Aktienmarktes – eine Zusammenfassung und Analyse empirischer Untersuchungen, Zeitschrift für betriebswirtschaftliche Forschung, 37, 500-518.

MONTIER, J., 2007. *Behavioral Investing – A practitioner's guide to applying behavioural fianance.* New York: John Wiley & Sons.

MORGENSTERN, O. AND VON NEUMANN, J., 1944. *Theory of Games and Economic Behavior.* Princeton: University Press.

MORLOCK, W., 1995. Stimmungs- und Liquiditätsindikatoren als Ratgeber für antizyklische Investments am deutschen Aktienmarkt. In: F. SCHMIELEWSKI, ed. Am Puls der Märkte – Moderne und bewährte Methoden der Kursdiagnostik. Frankfurt: Campus Verlag VTAD, 9-30.

MÖRSCH, J., 2005. Wissen ist Macht – Eine Analyse belegt: Unternehmensinsider schlagen mit ihren Aktienkäufen den Dax um Längen. Wie Anleger von den diskreten Geschäften profitieren. Insiderdeals. Capital, 18 August, p.104.

MOXTER, A., 1994. Grundsätze ordnungsmässiger Unternehmensbewertung. 2nd ed. Wiesbaden: Gabler.

MÜLLER, S. AND RÖDER K., 2001. Mehrperiode Anwendung des CAPM im Rahmen von DCF-Verfahren. Finanz Betrieb, 4, 225-233.

MURPHY, J.J., 1996. The Visual Investor – How to Spot Market Trends. New York: John Wiley & Sons.

MURPHY, J.J., 1999. Technical Analysis of the Financial Markets – A Comprehensive Guide to Trading Methods and Applications. New York: New York Institute of Finance.

MUTH, J. F., 1961. Rational Expectations and the Theory of Price Movements. Econometrica, 29, 315-335.

NEALE M.A. AND NORTHCRAFT, 1987. Experts, Amateurs, and Real Estate: An Anchoring-and-Adjustment Perspective on Property Pricing Decisions. Organizational Behavior and Human Decision Processes, 39, 84-97.

NIQUET, B., 1997. Der Crash der Theorien – Eine neue Sichtweise von Wirtschaft und Börse. Kulmbach: börsenbuchverlag.

ODEAN, T., 1998. Are Investors Reluctant to Realize Their Loses? The Journal of Finance, 53 (5), 1775-1798.

OEHLER, A., 2000. Behavioral Finance – Theoretische, empirische und experimentelle Befunde unter Marktrelevanz, Zeitschrift für das gesamte Bank- und Börsenwesen, 48 (11), 978-989.

OU, J.A. AND PENMAN, S.H., 1993. Financial Statement Analysis and the Evaluation of Market-to-Book Ratios. Working Paper. Santa Clara University.

PERKINS A.B. AND PERKINS M.C., 1999. *The Internet Bubble – Inside the Overvalued World of High-tech Stocks – and What You Need to Know to Avoid the Coming Shakeout.* New York: Harper Business.

PETERS. E.E., 1996. *Chaos and Order in the Capital Markets – A New View of Cycles, Prices, and Market Volatility.* 2nd ed. New York: John Wiley & Sons.

PETERSON, R.L., 2007. Inside the Investor's Brain – The Power of Mind Over Mondey. New York: John Wiley & Sons.

PLUMMER, T. 2006. *Forecasting Financial Markets – The Psychology of Successful Investing.* Philadelphia: Kogan Page.

POGET, S. AND WUERTH, A., 2007. Behavioral Finance ist ungenügend – Systemtheorie zeigt Beziehungen im Finanzmarkt – Kommunikation verbindet Investor, Unternehmen, Umfeld. Finanz und Wirtschaft, 25 April, p.43.

PRING, M.J., 1993. *Investment Psychology Explained – Classic Strategies to Beat the Markets.* New York: John Wiley & Sons.

PRING, M.J., 2002. *Technical Analysis Explained.* 4th ed. New York: McGraw-Hill.

PROKOP, J. AND ZIMMERMANN J., 2002. Unternehmensbewertung aus Sicht des Rechnungswesens – Das Residual Income Model. Wirtschaftswissenschaftliches Studium, 5, 272-277.

REIß, W., 1974. Random Walk Hypothese und deutscher Aktienmarkt. Thesis (PhD). University of Berlin.

ROSE, R., 2006. Enzyklopädie der Technischen Indikatoren – Trading-Chancen profitabel nutzen. Munich: FinanzBuch Verlag.

ROUWENHORST, K.G., 1997. International Momentum Strategies. The Journal of Finance, 53, 267-284.

ROUWENHORST, K.G., 1999. Local Return Factors and Turnover in Emerging Stock Markets. The Journal of Finance, 54, 1439-1464.

RÜBSAMEN, D., 2004. Technische Kumulationsanalyse. Munich: FinanzBuch Verlag.

RÜPPEL, W., 2005. Die Profis schauen auf den Sentix. Portfolio international, 1 March, p.42.

SAMUELSON, W. AND ZECKHAUSER, R., 1988. Status Quo Bias in Decision Making. Journal of Risk and Uncertainty, 1, 7-59.

SAPUSEK, A., 1998. Informationseffizienz auf Kapitalmärkten – Konzepte und empirische Ergebnisse. Wiesbaden: Gabler.

SCHÄFER, S.I. AND VATER, H., 2002. Behavioral Finance: Eine Einführung. Finanz Betrieb, 12, 739-748.

SCHIERECK, D. AND WEBER M., 1995. Zyklische und antizyklische Handelsstrategien am deutschen Aktienmarkt. Zeitschrift für betriebswirtschaftliche Forschung, 47, 3-24.

SCHIERECK D., 1999. Aktienhandel und Behavioral Finance. In: M. WEBER, ed. Behavioral Finance Group – Forschung für die Praxis. Mannheim: Lehrstuhl für ABWL, Finanzwirtschaft insbesondere Bankbetriebslehre University of Mannheim, Volume 1.

SCHIERECK D., 2000. Bleibe im Lande und rentiere dich kläglich: Der Home Bias. In: M. WEBER, ed. Behavioral Finance Group – Forschung für die Praxis. Mannheim: Lehrstuhl für ABWL, Finanzwirtschaft insbesondere Bankbetriebslehre University of Mannheim, Volume 9.

SCHMIDT, R. AND WULFF S., 1993. Zur Entdeckung von Insider-Aktivitäten am deutschen Aktienmarkt. Zeitschrift für Bankrecht und Bankwirtschaft, 5, 57-68.

SCHNEIDER, F., 2004. Wie Complin, CIO JPMorgan Fleming, die Erkenntnisse der Behavioral finance nutzt. Finanz und Wirtschaft, 18 August, p.37.

SCHWAGER, J.D., 1998. Schwager on Futures – Technische Analyse. 3rd ed. New York: John Wiley & Sons.

SEPIASHVILI, D., 2004. Expanding the usefullness of RSI. Futures, 33 (9), 34.

SEPPELFRICKE, P., 1999. Moderne Multiplikatorverfahren bei der Aktien- und Unternehmensbewertung. Finanz Betrieb, 10, 300-307.

SHEFRIN, H. AND STATMAN. M., 1985. The Disposition to Sell Winners Too Early and Ride Losers Too Long: Theory and Evidence. The Journal of Finance, 40, 777-792.

SHEFRIN, H., 2000. Börsenerfolg mit Behavioral Finance – Investment-Psychologie für Profis. Stuttgart: Schäfer-Poechel.

SHEFRIN, H., 2002. Beyond Greed and Fear – Understanding Behavioral Finance and the Psychology of Investing. Oxford: Oxford University Press.

SHILLER, R.J., 1981. Do Stock Prices Move Too Much to be Justified by Subsequent Changes in Dividends? American Economic Review, 71, 421-438.

SHILLER, R.J., 2000. Irrational Exuberance. Princeton: Princeton University Press.

SHLEIFER, A., 2000. *Inefficient Markets – An Introduction to Behavioral Finance.*
Oxford: Oxford University Press.

SOMMER, J., 1999. Künstliche neuronale Netze zur Beschreibung des
Anlegerverhaltens auf spekulativen Märkten: Eine theoretisch-experimentelle
Analyse. Thesis (PhD). University of Augsburg.

SORENSEN, E.H. AND WILLIAMSON, D.A., 1985. Some Evidence on the Value of
Dividend Discount Models. Financial Analysts Journal, 41 (11), 60-69.

SPREMANN, K., 2006. *Portfoliomanagement.* 3rd ed. Munich: Oldenbourg
Wissenschaftsverlag.

STAW, B.M., 1976. Knee-Deep in the Big Muddy: A Study of Escalating
Commitment to a Chosen Course of Action. Organizational Behavior and Human
Performance, 16, 27-44.

STEINER, M. AND WALLMEIER M., 1999. Unternehmensbewertung mit
Discounted Cash Flow-Methoden und dem Economic Value Added-Konzept.
Finanz Betrieb, 5, 1-10.

STOCK, D., 1990. Winner and Loser Anomalies in the German Stock Market.
Journal of Institutional and Theoretical Economics. 146, 518-529.

STOCK, D., 2001. Zur Tauglichkeit des Kurs-Gewinn-Verhältnisses für die
Prognose von Aktienkursveränderungen – eine Replik. Zeitschrift für
Betriebswirtschaft, 71 (3), 321-344.

STREITFERDT, F., 2008. Unternehmensbewertung mit den DCF-Verfahren nach
der Unternehmenssteuerreform 2008. Finanz Betrieb, 4, 268-276.

SUMMERS, L. H., 1986. Does Stock Market Rational Reflect Fundamental Values?
The Journal of Finance, 41, 591-601.

TVEDE, L., 2002. *The Psychology of Finance – Understanding the Behavioural Dynamics of Markets.* New York: John Wiley & Sons.

TVERSKY, A., 2004. *Preference, Belief, and Similarities.* Cambridge: MIT Press.

UHLIR, H., 1979. Überprüfung der Random-Walk-Hypothese auf dem Österreichischen Aktienmarkt. Thesis (PhD). University of Vienna.

VETTIGER, T. AND VOLKART, R., 2002. Kapitalkosten und Unternehmenswert – Zentrale Bedeutung der Kapitalkosten. Der Schweizer Treuhänder, 9, 751-758.

VIEKER, M., 1996. Indikatoren-Prognose – *Ökonometrische Untersuchungen zur Aktienprognose durch Technische Börsenindikatoren.* 2nd ed. Rosenheim: Thomas Müller Börsenverlag.

VOSSMANN, F., 1999. Aktienhandel und Behavioral Finance. In: M. WEBER, ed. Behavioral Finance Group – Forschung für die Praxis. Mannheim: Lehrstuhl für ABWL, Finanzwirtschaft insbesondere Bankbetriebslehre University of Mannheim, Volume 3.

WAUD, R. N., 1970. Public Interpretation of Federal Reserve Discount Rate Changes: Evidence on the "Announcement Effect". Econometrica, 38, 231-250.

WELCH, I., 2000. Herding among security analysts. Journal of Financial Economics, 58, 369-396.

WERMERS, R., 1999. Mutual Fund Herding and the Impact on Stock Prices. The Journal of Finance, 54 (2), 581-622.

WEST, K.D., 1988. Dividend Innovations and Stock Price Volatility. Econometrica, 56 (1), 37-61.

WHITE, R.W., 1959. Motivation Reconsidered: The Concept of Competence. Psychological Review, 66, 297-333.

WIDDEL, G., 1996. *Theorie und Praxis der Aktienspekulation: Strategien, Instrumente und Gewinnchancen.* Oldenburg: Oldenburg Verlag.

WILLIAMS, B., 1998. *New Trading Dimensions – How to Profit from Chaos in Stocks, Bonds, and Commodities.* New York: John Wiley & Sons.

ZIEG, K.C., 1997. *Point & Figure – Commodity & Stock Trading Techniques.* Greenville: Traders Press.

CPSIA information can be obtained
at www.ICGtesting.com
Printed in the USA
BVHW071043150221
600147BV00003B/324